SPIRITUAL HOSPITAL

Bible Studies Series 24

The
Power
in the
Blood
of
Jesus

Dr. D. K. Olukoya
General Overseer, MFM Ministries Worldwide

SPIRITUAL HOSPITAL - BIBLE STUDIES
THE POWER IN THE BLOOD OF JESUS
Series 24

ISSN: 0331 - 8583

Published by: Mountain of Fire and Miracles Ministries
International Headquarters, MFM Press
13, Olasimbo Street, Onike,
P. O. Box 2990, Sabo, Yaba,
Lagos, Nigeria.
Tel: 07014312988, 07016558981.

A CIP catalogue record of this book is available from the National Library.

CONTRIBUTORS TO THE BIBLE STUDIES

DKO
Pastor Kehinde
Pastor Adetayo
Pastor Gbesan
Pastor Yilu
Pastor Ajibade
Pastor Audu
Pastor Adesanya K.
Pastor Umoru
Pastor Laoye

Pastor Pius Oragwu
Pastor Uti
Pastor Ajila
Pastor Uche
Pastor F. K. Oladele
Pastor Ubong

INTRODUCTION REMARKS

Psalm 119:130: The entrance of thy words given light;
it giveth understanding unto the simple.

Glory be to the Most High, the Father of our Lord Jesus Christ. The Bible says "The Word of God is quick and powerful." The value of systematic Bible teaching in Christian Growth cannot be overemphasized.

This booklet has been complied from Bible Studies Outlines, used in our Monday spiritual Hospital Meetings, at the Mountain of Fire and Miracles Ministries International Headquarters in Lagos, Nigeria. It is presented to you here in its raw form, which will facilitate its use in group and general Bible studies. It would also offer a tremendous assistance in individual Bible Studies.

God bless you as you dig deep into the Word.

Yours in the School of Prayer,

Dr. D. K. Olukoya
General Overseer

TABLE OF CONTENT

LECTURE 1

...RODUCTION TO THE POWER IN THE BLOOD OF JESUS

MEMORY VERSE: John 6:53-56 Then Jesus said unto them, Verily, verily, I say unto you, Except ye eat the flesh of the Son of man, and drink his blood, ye have no life in you. Whoso eateth my flesh, and drinketh my blood, hath eternal life; and I will raise him up at the last day. For my flesh is meat indeed, and my blood is drink indeed. He that eateth my flesh, and drinketh my blood, dwelleth in me, and I in him.

TEXT: Hebrews 9

THE VALUE OF THE BLOOD

The Bible says: The life of flesh is in the blood...(Lev. 17:11). In other words, the blood is the source of life and that life is not just a physical life, but it is divine life. You will recall that in the book of Genesis when God made man and formed him out of the dust of the earth, man was just like a corpse having eyes, ears, nose, hands, legs, heart, etc., but n life. However, the Bible says, God breathed into man and man became a living soul (Genesis 2:7). That is to say man became a living entity - the eyes could see, the mouth could talk, the hands could move and the legs could carry him, all the organs could function perfectly because man had received the breath of life. So when God breathed into man, something happened. God transferred his divine life, His own life, His very life, He breathed into man.

The blood is the container of that life. Not our heart, lungs, stomach, liver, kidneys or such organs. The blood is the container or the retainer or the keeper of divine life. Human life is trapped in the blood. That is why in case of an accidental cut or gash on the body, the very first thing that is done is to make sure that the blood does not pour out. The flow of blood is stopped as early as possible because as blood flows out, life is also flowing out, although every other organ may remain intact.

When a man dies, the life that is contained in the blood goes back to God. What happens to the blood? Two or three hours after, the blood congeals. The blood ceases to flow because the life has gone out of it. It is the life in the blood that makes it to flow round the body. That is why at death, man is cold. Blood circulation ceases.

SALIENT POINTS

1. The human body is one of the greatest creations to ever exist. Designed and created by the Creator. Magnificent in origin, flawless in operation, amazing in study, and with an external soul. A soul that will live on forever someday.

2. Blood. The forgotten body system. Blood is an organ that we often do not acknowledge. A drop of blood just small enough to fill in the letter 'o' in your Bible contains 5 million red cells, 300,000 platelets and 7,000 white blood cells.

3. There is the pump. The heart. It beats on an average of 70 beats per minute or over 100,000 times in 24 hours. It ejects an average of 6 liters of blood every minute, 144 liters every day, 48,384 liters in a year, or in seventy years, 3,386,880 liters.

4. The heart requires no lubrication or maintenance. It nerve rests. It has an output that varies between .025 horsepower at rest and sleep and drives up to 1 horsepower in moments of stress. Its valves open and close 4,000 to 5,000 times each hour.

5. Sixty thousand miles of blood vessels are that pathway that the blood is limited to. Yet, the blood can be ejected from the heart and go to the heart and return in about twenty seconds.

6. It is blood that carries oxygen, nutrients, waste products, and fights infection all as the same time. And all of that just happened-Ps 139:4.

7. When the body begins to lose the flow of life, the blood pressure will drop and the heart will begin to strain to increase the output in an attempt to sustain the vital organs. IV fluids will work for a period of time to maintain that strain of blood of loss but there comes a point in which only blood is able to replace the loss. A transfusion is what is needed.

8. It was then that a clearer understanding came that life is indeed dependent on blood.

9. The Bible from its outset has always proved that blood is

significant for life, not so much the physical life but for eternal life. It is blood that has the power to cleanse sin. Exodus 12:13.

10. The flight from Egypt. The hustle to get ready in the dark. The preparation of the Passover Lamb. The blood applied to the door post. The mark of the blood was necessary for the first born to be saved. That is not without significance. There must be a mark of Calvary somewhere for you to be saved.

11. Throughout the Book, we find the word 'blood' 447 times in 375 different verses. It has numerous characteristics:
- It has a voice (Genesis 4:10 - Cain and Abel)
- It is the life (Genesis 9:4; Deut. 12:23)
- It cannot be concealed (Genesis 37:26)
- It has a mark when it is placed on things (Genesis 37:31)
- It can become judgment (Exodus 7:17-21)
- It may serve as a sign (Exodus 4:9)
- It is a token (Exodus 12:13)
- It seals a covenant (Exodus 24:8)

- It has specific requirements (Exodus 34:25)
- Only the chosen may use it (Leviticus 1:5)
- It places limitations (Leviticus 12:4-7)
- It is allowed to touch the Mercy Seat (Leviticus 16:15)
- It requires commitment (Leviticus 20:11-13)
- It serves as a sacrifice (Leviticus 7:33)
- It shows signs of injury (Deut 32:42)
- It is a sign of peace (2 Kings 16:13)
- It is precious (Psalm 92:14)

12. Yet, the blood of Jesus Christ is greater:
- It is the redeemer of sins (Matthew 26:28)
- His blood is just and innocent (Matt 27:24)
- It was shed for many (Mark 14:24)
- It has eternal life (John 6:54)
- It came out of His side (John 19:34)
- It is a declaration of righteousness (Romans 3:25)
- It has the power to justify (Romans 5:9)
- It has to be taken in communion (1 Cor 10:16)

- It has the power to condemn (1 Cor 11:27)
- It supplies redemption (Eph. 1:7; Col. 1:!4; Heb 9:12)
- It brings us close to Him (Eph 2:13)
- It supplies peace (Col. 1:20)
- It destroys the power of death (Heb 2:14)
- It purges the conscience (Heb 9:14)
- It supplies boldness (Heb 10:19)
- It is the sign of an everlasting covenant (Heb 13:20)

- It is precious (1 Peter 1:19)
- It cleanses (1 John 1:7)
- It washes away sin (Rev 1:5)
- It provides whiteness (Rev. 7:14)
- It is an overcomer (Rev. 12:11)
13. That is what the power of the blood can do.

CONCLUSION: There is power in the blood of Jesus to save, to heal and to deliver.

PRAYER POINT: Blood of Jesus, arise in the thunder of Your power and speak for me and fight for me.

LECTURE 2
WHY SATAN IS AFRAID OF THE BLOOD OF JESUS

MEMORY VERSE: "And they overcame him by the blood of the lamb and by the word of their testimony, and they loved not their loves unto the death." Rev. 12:11.

TEXTS: Gen. 4:10, Ex. 12, Col. 1:14-20, Heb. 9:6-28.

INTRODUCTION

The Blood of Jesus is an awesome Blood. It is not comparable to the Blood of any man dead or alive. Lev. 17:11. Says "For the life of the flesh is in the Blood." Likewise the Life of Jesus was and forever is in His Blood, his Holy nature; Power and Wisdom are contained in His Blood. The Blood of Jesus is the ultimate Power of Victory. His Blood scares the devil to his bones.

The Blood of Jesus guarantees man's access to God, and through His Precious Blood we receive life and power to live in unquestionable dominion above all unpleasant situations and challenges of life.

SEVEN FOLD SHEDDING OF BLOOD OF JESUS

1. Sweated drops of Blood in the Garden of Gethsemane - Lk. 22:44.
2. He bled from beating He received on His face - Lk. 22.
3. He bled from having his beard plucked out - Isa. 50:6.
4. He bled from the brutal scourging. His back and abdomen were lacerated - Matt. 27:26.
5. He bled from the crown of thorns crushed on His Head - Matt. 27:9.
6. He bled from nails driven through His Hands - Lk. 23:33.
7. He bled from a Roman Spear that pierced through His Heart - Jn. 19:34.

THE BLESSINGS WE RECEIVE BY HIS SEVEN GOLD BLEEDING

1. We receive protection by the Blood of Jesus - Ex.12:13.
2. Salvation comes through the Blood of Jesus - Mk. 14:24, Acts 4:12.
3. Healing is provided by the Blood - Isa. 5:35.
4. Financial and marital blessings are released through the Blood of Jesus - Ps. 105:24,37.
5. Abundant life is given by the Blood of Jesus - Jn. 10:10.

6. Forgiveness of sins comes through the Blood of Jesus - Heb. 9:22.
7. Thorough cleaning is accomplished through the Blood of Jesus - 1 Jn. 1:7.
8. Total redemption comes through the Blood - Eph. 1:7.
9. We are justified by His Blood - Rom. 5:9.
10. We are sanctified by His precious Blood - Heb. 13:12.
11. We received peace through the Blood of Jesus - Col. 1 :19-20.
12. We receive overcomers' power from His Blood - Rev. 12:11
13. We receive greater and better things than old Testament saints through His Blood - Heb. 12:24.
14. We are given access into the Holiest of all by the Blood of Jesus - Heb. 10:19.

WHY SATAN FEARS THE BLOOD OF JESUS

1. Satan fears the Blood of Jesus because he cannot solve the mystery of the shedding of Blood on the Cross - Col. 2:14-15.
2. The devil fears the Blood of Jesus because he cannot create a counterfeit blood.
3. Satan fears the Blood of Jesus it is the proof and evidence of his defeat and doom.
4. The devil fears the Blood of Jesus because JESUS did a complete JOB at Calvary. Nothing remains to be done. His precious Blood is more than sufficient to cleanse all the sins of mankind. One drop of the Blood of Jesus is enough to destroy Satan's kingdom.
5. Satan fears the Blood of Jesus because it has power that draws us closer to God. We were once far away from God have been brought near by the Blood of Jesus.
6. The devil is afraid of the Blood of Jesus because it gives us power to tread upon serpents and scorpions and upon all the powers of the enemy - Lk. 10:19.
7. Satan is afraid of the Blood of Jesus because it strengthens our faith.
8. Satan fears the Blood of Jesus because it fortifies us against his evil arrows and fiery darts.
9. The Blood of Jesus amplifies and gives life to our prayers.

10.The Blood of Jesus moves Heaven and Earth on our behalf for the fulfilment of God's purposes.

11.The Blood of Jesus provides dominion over sin.

12.We are saved, delivered, healed and blessed forever by the Awesome Blood of Jesus.

13.The devil fears the Blood of Jesus because every time we shout the "BLOOD OF JESUS" we are invoking the Glory of God.

14.The devil fears the Blood of Jesus because the life and power of Jesus is in His Blood – Lev. 17:11.

15.Anytime we plead the BLOOD OF JESUS God takes over our battles and fights for us.

16.The Blood of Jesus was and is the Passover Blood of the Lamb of God. When you plead the Blood of Jesus. The angel of death will Passover you, your families and your properties – Ex. 12:24-25, Jn. 1:36.

IN CONCLUSION: The major reasons so many of us are living defeated lives as Christians is because we have never. Learned to apply the Blood of Jesus to our circumstances to bring – deliverance, healing and wholeness to our lives.

The Blood of Jesus has the ability to speak and intercede on our behalf before the throng of Grace and Mercy. Bust so often we do not take the advantage of that benefit either out of ignorance or unbelief.

Before you go to bed at night plead the Blood of Jesus. Every morning when you wake up, cover yourself, your family, your business, your journey with the Blood of Jesus and you will be protected and secured from the torture and afflictions of the wicked.

PRAYER: By the Power in the Blood of Jesus, I trample upon serpents and scorpions and upon all the powers of the enemy and nothing shall by any means hurt me, in the name of Jesus.

LECTURE 3
THE CYCLE OF THE BLOOD

MEMORY VERSE: And thou shalt smite the house of Ahab thy master, that I may avenge the blood of my servants the prophets, and the blood of all the servants of the LORD, at the hand of Jezebel. 2 Kings 9:7

TEXTS: Gen. 42:19-23; Luke 11:49-50; Lev. 20:9-22.

INTRODUCTION

God created man in His own image. He made man a living soul with the breath of life which is the blood, blood became an essence of life Gen.9:4. No man is expected to take another man's blood or stain another because that blood comes from God to man and back to God. Whosoever shadeth man's blood shall his blood be shed Gen. 9:6.

SALIENT POINTS ABOUT THE CYCLE

➤ The cycle is referred to the flow or blood pressure that occurs from the beginning of one heart beat to the beginning of the next.

➤ A cycle is completed when the heart fills with blood and the blood is pumped from the heart.

➤ The heart pumps blood continually without taking a break and it is estimated that a given portion of blood will take 30 seconds to complete one course with the heart values opening and closing in response to the blood pressure.

➤ The avenged heart beats about 75 times per minutes and each heart cycle takes about 0.8 seconds to compete.

SCRIPTURAL WARNING ABOUT THE CYCLE OF THE BLOOD

The blood of Jesus is precious, clean it serves as a sacrifice. It has eternal life and greater than any other blood. It is the life, it has a voice and cannot be concealed. This is why the scripture warns against the shedding of the blood unjustly because it will hunt the slayer to bring judgement from generation to generation.

a. Thou shall not stand against the blood of thy neighbour (Lev. 19:16)

b. Ye shall eat the blood of no manner of flesh (Lev. 17:14).

c. Thou shall not shed the blood of another man (Gen. 9:6)

d. Thou shall not pollute the land with blood for blood defileth the land (Num. 35:33).

e. Delight not in the blood of the bullocks (Isaiah 1:11)

f. Pollution of blood brings iniquity (Hosea 6:8).

g. Avoid building your city with blood because it shall be required from your generation (Micah 3:10).

h. Fear, unrest will always pursue men slayers (Hab. 2:17).

i. Shedding the blood of the saints brings everlasting punishment on the generation (Rev. 16:6)

j. Pestilence, diseases, sicknesses and death and the products of unjust shedding of blood (Ezek. 28:23).

k. By the power in the blood of Jesus every knee shall bow with the blood of Jesus.

WHEN DOES THE BLOOD BECOME A CYCLE?

1. When watchmen see the sword come and blow not the trumpet (Ezek. 33:3).

2. When you fail to warn the wicked (Ezek. 33:8).

3. When you refuse to yield to warning (Ezek. 33:4).

4. When you slay the innocent (Luke 11:51, 2 King 24:4).

5. When you contribute to kill the righteous (Luke 11:51).

6. When you do prophets of God harm or kill them.

7. When you are eating blood (Lev. 19:26).

8. When you contribute to kill a stranger (Lev. 19:34).

9. When you judge unrighteously.

10. When you rein curses upon your father and your mother (Lev. 20:9).

11. When you commit adultery with another man's wife (Lev. 20:10).

12. When you lie with your father's wife (Lev. 20:11).

13. When you lie with both mother and daughter (Lev. 20:17)

14. If a man or woman lie with a beast (Lev. 20:16).

15. When you lied with your father or mother.

16. If you have ever offered sacrifices to gods using blood.

17. When you steal what does not belong to you.

18. When you steal from God or eat God's money.

19. When you embezzle God's money.
20. When you lead someone to destruction or disaster.
21. When you cover your sin.
22. When you tell lies to destroy others.
23. When you cheat others.

SOME ADVANTAGES OF THE CYCLE OF THE BLOOD

1. It gives life (Deut. 12:23).
2. Gives us a better covenant (Zech. 9:11).
3. Brings revelation (Matt. 16:17).
4. Ensures righteous (Matt. 23:20).
5. Brings signs and wonders (Acts 2:19).
6. It strengthens our faith (Rom. 3:25).
7. It cleanses our sins (Acts 20:28).
8. Brings total healing and deliverance (Heb. 12:24).
9. Causes revival (1 John 5:8).
10. Ensures long and better life.

CONCLUSION
The flow of blessings of God can be continuous if it is not terminated. The righteous ensures better life, healing deliverance and unbelievable victory. The cycle must be grounded and avoid every evil breaker or destroyer. The blood of Jesus will always be there build and reached those ask.

PRAYER
1. Lord empower and fulfil my destiny, in the name of Jesus.
2. Let the glory of God over shadow every one and the land, in the name of Jesus.

LECTURE 4
THE BLOODLINE

MEMORY VERSE: "...and when I see the blood, I will pass over you..." (Exod 12: 13)

TEXTS: Exod. 12: 1-13; Rev. 5: 9-10

INTRODUCTION

In looking at this topic, there are two words added together – Blood and line.

What is blood? Blood is that fluid in human body that moves throughout the entire human body and supply the fixed cells with nourishment and carry off the waste products from them. In the normal body, there are about 5 quarts of this fluid and this blood is pumped by the heart circulates throughout the body system about every twenty-three seconds so that every cell in the body is constantly supplied and cleansed.

The blood is the most mysterious of all the tissues in the body system. The Bible says in Lev 17:11 "For the life of the flesh is in the blood".

Now what is line? Line is can be defined as: an edge, a border, a demarcation, a separation.

WHAT IS THE BLOODLINE?

Scripturally speaking, the authority of the bloodline can be clearly seen in the example of the Egyptian plagues we read in our text.

The Lord told Moses how children of Israel would be spared from the death of the first born. They were told to follow these seven instructions:

1. Choose a one year old lamb or goat without blemish (Ex 12: 3-5)
2. Join together with small families that cannot use a whole lamb (Ex 12:4)
3. Keep the lamb for few days before slaughter (Ex 12:6)
4. Have the head of the household slay the lamb on the evening of the fourteenth day of the month (Ex 12:6)
5. Sprinkle the blood of the lamb on the sides and tops of the door frames of the house (Ex 12:7)
6. Roast the Lamb that evening and eat it with bitter herbs and unleavened bread (Ex 12: 8)
7. Eat the meal in haste with their cloaks tucked into their belts, sandals on their feet and staves in their hands (Ex 12:11)

God told them to prepare because He would pass over the land (Ex 12:12). And the Lord gave them a promise in Ex 12:12.

A blood line spiritually can be described as:

a. The line of demarcation between the children of God and those who are separated and alienated God.
b. A sign of protection over the children of God from all evils. (Psalm 91: 10)
c. A line of division, separating the children of God from disasters and calamity (Ps 91: 7).

Today, the blood of Jesus Christ that speaks better things than the blood of Abel stands as our bloodline.

WHAT IS THE IMPORTANCE OF THE BLOODLINE?

1. The bloodline designates the family of God - Romans 5:9
2. The bloodline divides - Ex 12:23
3. The bloodline protects - Ex 12: 29 - 30
4. The bloodline defends
5. The bloodline delivers.
6. The bloodline provides salvation - Romans 5:9; Eph 1:7

7. The bloodline provides an hedge around a believer - Job 1: 7 - 10

WHAT ARE THE CONDITIONS NECESSARY TO ACTIVATE THE BLOODLINE?

1. You must surrender your life to Jesus Christ.
2. You live a holy life
3. You must believe in faith
4. On daily basis cover yourself, your household and everything concerning you with the blood of Jesus.

CONCLUSION

For all other men who had been crucified, their stories ended when their hearts stopped beating. There was nothing left to do but retrieved and buried their bodies. But Jesus Christ was not any other man. He was the Son of God. There had never been another man like this God-man nor would there ever be another like Him.

The blood of sprinkling of Jesus Christ speaks better things than the blood of Abel. The Bloodline of Jesus Christ speaks, mercy, forgiveness, reconciliation, deliverance, protection and healing. Apply it today in obedience and it shall defend you in Jesus name, Amen.

LECTURE 5
THE BLOOD OF THE COVENANT

MEMORY VERSE: "Then he took the cup and gave thanks and gave it to them, saying, drink from it, all of you. For this is my blood of the new covenant which is shed for many for the remission of sins." Matt 26:27-28.

TEXTS: Hebrews 9:11-15

INTRODUCTION

The blood of Jesus is our covenant connector, when Jesus said on the cross "It is finished" he was referring to the Abrahamic covenant being available to everyone by faith believes in his blood. The blood of the new covenant is not just some other form of a covenant, rather it is the most high covenant available and it is backed up by God himself. This covenant brings man into communion and unity with God. In this covenant we become partakers of God's character or his divine nature. John 17:21-22.

WHAT IS THE BLOOD OF THE COVENANT?
1. It is the blood of sacrifice
2. The bible is a book of blood and the blood of the covenant is the message of the bible both in Old and New Testaments.

3 It is a miracle fluid that only God could make.

4 In the Old Testament, it is a testimonial sacrifice proclaiming the coming of the true lamb of God.

5 In the Old Testament, it covers the sins of the worshipper.

6 In the Old Testament, it points to the precious blood of the lamb of God.

7 The blood of Jesus Christ is the ultimate blood of the covenant between God and man. John 1:17,Heb 8:4-9

8 The blood of the covenant is the sacrifice of the highest value. John 10:17-18

9 It is the purest sacrifice. John 8:46, 1Pet 2:22

10 It is the substitutionary sacrifice. 2Corth 5:21, 1Pet 3:18

11 It is a Passover sacrifice. 1Cor 5:7

12 It is the life of our Lord Jesus Christ, giving up his life for us.

13 It is the basis of life and the shedding of the blood stands for the end of life. Luke 11:50-51

14 It is an indication of violent death.

15 It is fulfillment of God's purpose of salvation expressed in the covenant of the Old testament, mediated by Jesus Christ sealed in his blood.

16 It is a price paid for grace.

HOW JESUS PAID THE PRICE OF THE COVENANT WITH HIS BLOOD

1 Agony of his soul Luke 22:44
2 Betrayal Luke 22:3,48
3 Beaten and mocked Luke 22:64
4 Falsely condemned to death Mk 15:13, John 19:6
5 Cruelly Scourged
6 Ridiculed and abused Mt 27:29-31
7 Crucified Luke 23:34-39
8 Burdened with the weight of sin

THE POWER OF THE BLOOD OF THE COVENANT

1 It is a speaking blood and when it speaks:
A broken heart is healed.
B The troubled conscience is at rest.
C The tormenting soul is silenced.
D The rage of darkness is quenched.

2 Jesus is our high priest of the covenant.
3 Our intercessor, mediator and advocate is Jesus.
4 Our victory now and eternity is guarantee. Rev 19:11, 12:11
5 It is a blood line that separates the goat and the sheep. Matt 25:31-32
6 It propels to obedience.
7 Pleading the blood is a legal, rightful duty of a believer in Christ. It is involving what Jesus has done on the cross over a particular situation or person.
8 The power of this blood is the only antidote for any evil covenants.

WHEN TO APPLY THE BLOOD OF THE COVENANT

1 When the devil tries to torment us with the memory of negative past
2 When we want to break free from evil and destructive habit
3 When we want to break all forms evil patterns
4 When we intend to rise above above our demonic roots or foundations
5 When we desire healings in our body, soul and spirit.

6 When our dreams are becoming battle field

7 When the enemies try to weaken our faith

8 When we sense dangers in our environment

9 When we are at our wit end and desire urgent divine intervention

10 When we are faced with stubborn enemies and problem expanders

11 When we are breaking multiple covenants and curses

12 When we intend to silence evil mockers and dangerous accusers.

13 When your enemies seem to be stronger than you

14 When your case has been declared impossible

15 When you desperately desire a change in your situation.

BENEFITS OF THE BLOOD OF THE COVENANT

1 By the blood of the covenant, we receive the remission and forgiveness of sin. Matt 26:28

2 We are completely washed of our sins. Rev 1:5

3 We are redeemed. Eph 1:7, Colos 1:14

4 We are justified, regarded as innocent before God. Rom 5:9

5 We are brought near to God. Eph 2:13

6 We have peace with God. Colos 1:20

7 We are cleansed in our conscience. Heb 9:14

8 We are made holy and set apart for God. Heb 13:12

9 We will have new boldness to approach God and ask for his help. Heb 10:19

10 We can have ongoing cleansing from sin. 1John 1:17

11 We will overcome the enemy. Rev 12:11

12 We are made conscious of righteousness rather than sin.

13 We are set free from dead works so that we serve the living God.

14 We receive testimony of diverse kinds; healing, sound mind, deliverance etc.

15 We are completely set free from Satan, the world and self.

16 Our faith in God receives boosting.

17 We are strengthened.

18 We receive eternal life

19 We receive boldness to come into God's presence.

20 We are brought back into fellowship with God.

21 Our minds are purged from the past and present sins. Heb 10:21-22

22 We receive divine protection

23 The blood of the covenant is our vital link to God.

HOW TO MAKE THE BLOOD OF THE COVENANT WORK FOR YOU

1 It must be applied with the understanding that God cannot and will never break his covenant. Ps 89:34, Jer 33:20-21

2 We must dwell in God's secret place, which refers to being born again. Ps 91:1

3 We must confess it, say it and keep saying it until it yields result and never stop saying it. Ps 91:2 whatever you cannot say, you cannot have.

4 We must love God above all things, this includes our desire to please him always. God cannot bless you more than the level of your love towards him.

5 You need a daily renewal of your mind, spending time in the covenant through systematic and consistent study of the word of God.

6 Beware of and avoid depression. Depression hinders your flight to your places in the covenant of the blood. Heb 3:17-19

7 Endeavour to walk within the covenant with God, only his agreement with you guarantee his walk with you.

8 At all times, stand in the covenant of the blood.

9 Call him, trust him, fear him and praise him all the time

CONCLUSION

As believers, we must know the significance and the power of Jesus's blood as well as how to appropriate it in our lives. Doing so positions us to experience the reality of the blessing Jesus death and resurrection gives to us. The blood of the new covenant must not be overlooked but rather tapping or connecting into the mystery will make us victorious and successful all the days of our lives.

PRAYER POINTS

1 By the blood of Jesus, this hour, I break forever all satanic covenants and curses limiting my destiny in the name of Jesus.

2 By the blood of Jesus, I rise above my roots in Jesus name.

3 Where is the Lord God of Elijah, arise by the power in the blood of Jesus and make a way for me.

LECTURE 6
THE BLOOD AS A LIFE GIVER

TEXT: 1Pet. 1:18-21; John 6:54; Eph. 2:13; Heb. 12:24; Rev. 12:11; Heb. 10:29; 1John 5:6-7; Col. 1:19-22; Heb. 9:22.

MEMORY VERSE: John 6:53.

A. INTRODUCTION

The blood of Jesus shed at Golgotha is an eternal sacrifice that can never lose its potency. It comes with the package of healing, salvation and deliverance, because it is the blood of a sinless, selfless and compassionate saviour. By the shedding of the blood on the cross, man is able to move from condemnation to redemption and giving us life instead of death. Our sinful nature and generational sins, condemns us to death, both spiritually and physically. The love of God gave us redemption and opportunity for life eternal. Satan holds the law as his legal primary weapon against man, but the grace of God, by the perfect work of salvation and redemption, reconciles man from damnation, making our spirit alive unto God presently and in the resurrection.

B. FACTS ABOUT THE BLOOD

1. There is no substitution for blood.
2. 7% of the body weight is blood.
3. The blood carries oxygen to all parts of the body.
4. The blood distributes nutrients gotten from food to the body.
5. Waste products like carbon dioxide are removed from the body through the blood.
6. The blood fights infections.
7. Healing of wounds is done by the blood.
8. There are four main types of blood; A, B AB and O.
9. One out of ten people, entering the hospital, require blood transfusion.

C. WHAT MAKES THE BLOOD OF CHRIST A LIFE GIVER

1. Christ's divine conception; Matt. 1:20.
2. Christ's humble lifestyle; Phil. 2:6-11.
3. He was a holy seed in the womb; Luke 1:35.
4. He lived a sinless life; Heb. 4:15.
5. Holy circumcision; Col. 2:11.

6. He voluntarily offered Himself; Heb. 9:28.
7. He is our great High Priest; Heb. 3:1.
8. His destiny was to give His life and give us life; Matt. 1:21.
9. He was a man of great compassion; Mark 8:2.
10. It was a holy and spiritual sacrifice; Heb. 9:14.
11. It was a holy blood that was offered.
12. It is the blood of the renewed covenant.
13. He is the only begotten Son of the Father; John 1:14.

D. THOSE WHO CANNOT RECEIVE LIFE IN THE BLOOD OF JESUS

1. Those who have not encountered Jesus.
2. Those who reject the gospel.
3. Those who refuse to confess their sins.
4. Those who gamble at the cross.
5. Those who run away from the Lord's Supper.
6. The proud and boastful.
7. Those who hate their fellow brethren.
8. Those who do not agree that Jesus is the Messiah and Saviour of the world.
9. Those who have confessed to Jesus, but have not repented.
10. Those not yet convicted by the Holy Ghost.
11. Those attacking the church of God from within.
12. Those drinking the water of fornication and adultery.
13. Those whose tongues have confessed Jesus but still tell lies and use their mouth to destroy their fellow brethren.
14. Those whose hearts do not convict them when they sin.
15. Those who are now over familiar with God and His servants.
16. Those who have become stumbling blocks in the house of God.
17. Those who harbour unforgiveness in their hearts.
18. The clever and wilful sinners.
19. Those that the love of money has replaced the love of God in their hearts.

E. THE POWER OF LIFE IN THE BLOOD OF JESUS

1. Redemption; 1Pet. 1:18-19, Eph. 1:7-8.
2. Healing; Isa. 53:5.
3. Restoration.

4. Reconciliation.
5. Protection; Ex. 12:13.
6. Deliverance; Rev. 12:11.
7. Justification; Rom. 5:16.
8. New birth; 2Cor. 5:17.
9. Forgiveness; Acts 13:37-38.
10. Breaks the power of sin; Rev. 1:5-6.
11. Destroys curses and covenants; Gal. 3:13-14.
12. Sanctification; Heb. 10:14.
13. Cleanses conscience; Heb. 9:13-14.
14. Freedom from fear; Rom. 8:9-17.
15. R e n e w e d   d i v i n e communication; Heb. 10:19-21.
16. Grace of God or unmerited favour from God.
17. Victory; Rev. 19:11-13.

F. **HOW TO BENEFIT FROM THE LIFE IN THE BLOOD OF JESUS**
1. Repentance.
2. Conversion.
3. Be a lover of the word.
4. Regularly commit yourself to God in prayer.
5. Never cover up any sin as God sees it as pride when you refuse to confess your sin.
6. Never absent yourself from the gathering of the children of God.

7. Strive to live a life of holiness
8. Pleading the blood of Jesus over your mind to prevent evil thoughts.
9. Break fellowship with anyone that causes you to sin

G. **APPLICATION OF THE BLOOD AS A LIFE GIVER**
1. By pleading the blood of Jesus.
2. Drinking the blood of Jesus.
3. By soaking yourself in the blood of Jesus.
4. Holy Communion which helps to renew the covenant of the cross
5. Regular confession of the blood of Jesus as atonement for your sin.
6. Applying the blood of Jesus on sicknesses and infirmities.

H. **CONCLUSION**
Although 2000 years ago, the blood was shed, yet it speaks better things than the blood of Abel, speaking life and killing death. Grace, mercy and abundant life eternal is released through the blood of Jesus that has made a way back for us to the Living God.

I. **PRAYER POINT**
1. Oh Lord, let the blood of Jesus avail for me in every area of my life, in Jesus name.

LECTURE 7
THE BLOOD THAT SPEAKS

MEMORY VERSE: "And to Jesus the mediator of the new covenant, and to the blood of sprinkling, that speaketh better things than that of Abel." Heb. 12:24.

TEXTS: Heb. 12:22-25, 28-29; Heb. 12:11-13

INTRODUCTION

Blood has power. Life is in the Blood. The Blood of Jesus has superior power. It has The Voice that exercises the Ultimate Power both in heaven, on earth and under the earth (i.e. in hell). All the creation submits to this blood. The blood of Jesus Christ silences every other voice. The power in that blood terrorises and exterminates every opposition. Today the children of God MUST arise in power and begin to make greater and more excellent use of this blood of Jesus Christ which is freely given to us, for our ultimate victory on earth and in eternity.

BIBLE OBSERVATIONS

1. Life is in the blood. Therefore blood must not be eaten or wrongly handed – Deut. 12:23-25.

2. Shedding of innocent blood speaks VENGEANCE for the earth. This is very dangerous – Gen. 4:9-12.

3. God hates witches because they drink blood – Exo. 22:18.

4. Human sacrifice is abomination to god and attracts the anger of God, with terrible punishment – Lev. 18:21; Deut. 18:10; Ezek. 20:31.

5. The demons require blood sacrifice so that they can taste the life in the blood. This must be seriously shunned – Jer. 32:35.

6. The devil tried to hinder Jesus Christ from growing up to fulfil the ministry of shedding His blood for the remission of our sins – Jer. 31:15; Matt. 2:7-8, 12, 16-18.

7. The shedding of blood was require to cover sins in the Old Testament – Gen. 21; Heb. 10:1-8.

8. Without shedding of blood, sins cannot be paid for – Heb. 9:22.

9. The blood of Jesus Christ washes away sins completely – Heb. 9:11-16.

10. The power in the blood of Jesus Christ will keep on fighting for the children of God until the end of time – Rev. 12:9-11.

WHOM SHALL THE BLOOD OF JESUS CHRIST SPEAK IN FAVOUR OF?

1. Those who are born again – Jn. 1:12.
2. Those for whom other believers are praying on their behalf making use of the blood of Jesus Christ – Ezek. 22:23-31.
3. Those who have the knowledge of how to use the blood – Jn. 8:31-32.
4. Those who apply the power of this blood to all the situations of their lives – Rev. 12:11.
5. Those who walk in the light of God – 1 Jn. 1:7.
6. Those who confess their sins to God and repent from them – 1 Jn. 8:9.

HOW TO MAKE THE BLOOD OF JESUS CHRIST SPEAK FOR YOU

1. Repent from all your sins.
2. Accept Jesus Christ into your heart as your Lord and personal Saviours – Jn. 3:16.
3. Receive the Holy Spirit baptism – Acts 1:8; Acts 2:1-4.
4. Become a Bible addict – Josh. 1:8; Ps. 119:9-11.

5. Always attend Christian fellowships and Bible believing churches – Heb. 10:25.
6. Make yourself a faithful witness of the love of God – tell others what Christ means to you and has done for you – Matt. 28:18-20.
7. Always bear the fruit of the Holy Spirit, i.e., godly Christian character – Gal. 5:22-26.
8. Provoke others to love God – Heb. 10:24.
9. Become a prayer addict and warrior – Eph. 6:18; 1 Thess. 5:17.
10. Always apply and plead the blood of Jesus Christ over every area of your life, family and ministry – Rev. 12:10.

CONCLUSION: The Blood of Jesus Christ still speaks powerfully today. It is one of the greatest weapons available to us in this Christian journey and warfare. You MUST not take this Blood for granted if you desire permanent and continuous victory. When you feel weak in your body, soak it in the Blood of Jesus Christ. Soak your family in this Blood. It neutralises every evil power. Soak your habitation in this Blood. Learn to drink this Blood always. It heals all sicknesses. Faithful use of this Blood of Jesus Christ will usher you into dumbfounding victories and progress. This shall be your experience from now and forever in the Almighty name of our Lord and Saviour Jesus Christ. Amen.

Chorus to sing:

I plead the blood, the blood of Jesus
I drink the blood, the blood of Jesus
I am covered in the blood, the blood of Jesus.

PRAYER POINTS

1. Blood of Jesus Christ, arise, fight for me, in Jesus' name.

2. Blood of Jesus Christ, catapult me into divine greatness, in Jesus' name.

LECTURE 8
EAT MY FLESH AND DRINK MY BLOOD

MEMORY VERSE:- John 6:54-
Whoso eatheth my flesh and
drinketh my blood hath eternal life:
and I will raise him up at the last
day.

TEXT: Jn. 6:32-33; Jn. 14:6; 53-58,
Jn. 6:35.

BACKGROUND:
John 6:35-"And Jesus said unto
them, I am the bread of life, he that
cometh to me shall never hunger,
and he that believeth on me shall
never thirst".

- The background to this
  statement is the feeding of the
  5000
- At the end of this feeding, they
  wanted to take Jesus by force
  and make him King.
- Jesus had left them to go across
  Galilee
- They followed him and came to
  the other side
- Jesus accused them of following
  Him only to satisfy their empty
  belies
- Men often use religion for
  physical gain.
- Indeed the people demanded
  that He show them another
  Miracle.

- The people are concerned with
  physical and material things
  while Jesus was teaching them
  hard spiritual issue.

INTRODUCTION

The statement Eat my Flesh
and Drink my Blood must
be understood as a
figurative expression rather than its
literal meaning. Jesus Christ is fully
aware that drinking of blood is
prohibited and cannot introduce
cannibalism. The Jews were
familiar with eating and drinking
being used figuratively in the Old
Testament to describe the
appropriation of divine blessings to
one's innermost being. It was God's
way of providing spiritual
nourishment for the Soul. Is. 55:1-
3, Ezekiel. 2:8, 3:1.

(1) Students of the Bible know that
at times Jesus spoke in
Parables-Figuratively and at
times plainly.
(2) The Gospel of John records 8
figuratively declarations Jesus
made of Himself.
The Bread of Life-Jn. 6:48;
(2) The Light of the Word- Jn
8:12
(3) The Door Jn. 10:9.

(4) The Good Shepherd-Jn. 10:11

(5) The Resurrection and the life Jn. 11:25.

(6) The way, the Truth and the life -Jn. 14:6 and

(7) The True Vine Jn. 15:1;

(8) He also referred to His body as the temple -Jn. 2:19.

The words were purely spiritual. In Jn. 6:63. It is the spirit that quickeneth, the flesh profiteth nothing, the words that I speak unto you they are spirit and they are life.

These statement is spiritual and symbolic not in the literal sense at all.

For example if a Football Coach says "Men in the next three months, you are going to eat, drink and breathe football". This simply means that the three months would be absolutely devoted to football.

Jesus is telling all of us that for the rest of our lives he must be central to our lives.

He is talking about the only process by which we enter into a saving relationship with Him.

SPECIFIC MEANING OF THE PHRASE

-1- Was talking about enjoying the benefits which come from His death

-2- He stressed that we cannot go long without a drink because liquid is vital for our bodies and food is something we need moment by moment to sustain us.

-3- In the book of John- A branch cut away from the vine is cut away from the cap. That source of nourishment and fluid flowing up and down would die straight away. We must be joined to Christ and constantly feed from Him and draw substance from him in order to be sustained.

-4- The eating and drinking results in everlasting life Jn. 6:27- Do not labour for the food which perished but for the food which endures to everlasting life which the Son of man will give you.

- We can also think of the woman of Samaria who was told in Jn. 4:14 that drinking the water that clush offers would lead to everlasting life.

-5- This also means that believing also leads to everlasting life- Jn. 3:16.-Jn. 6:40.

-6- It means coming to Jesus -Jn.6:35;Jn. 7:37

-7- It means obeying/abiding in the words of Christ.

THE SIGNIFICANCE OF THE STATEMENT "I AM"

This is significant because they gave an understanding of the relationship we need to have with Jesus.

-1- He and He alone is the bread of life

-2- He is the one who gives the meat that leads to eternal life- Jn. 6:27

-3- He is the true bread from heaven-Jn. 6:32

-4- He is the bread that gives life to the world-Jn. 6:33

-5- He is the bread of life-Jn. 6:35, 48.

-6- He promises to quell our hunger and quench our thirst - Jn. 6:35

-7- He provides the bread of which those who eat will not die- Jn. 6:50 & 51

-8- He is the living bread which came down from heaven -Jn. 6:51

-9- He is the one who gives his flesh, which is the bread, for the life of the world. Jn.6:51

-10- He is the one who gives his flesh and blood for meat and drink - Jn. 6:54,55

-11- He is the one who dwells in the one who eats his flesh and drinks his blood-Jn. 6:56

-12- He is the one in whom the one who eats and drinks his blood dwells. -Jn. 6:56

THE SIGNIFICANCE OF THE BLOOD OF JESUS

The significance and efficacy of the shed blood of Jesus indicates that the blood of Jesus relates to

1. Redemption Acts 20:28, Eph. 1:7,1Pt.1:19, Rev. 5:9
2. Propitiation-Rom. 3:25
3. Cleansing -Heb.9:14, 1Jn. 1:7, Rev. 7:14
4. Forgiveness- Eph. 1:7, Heb.
5. Access to God- Eph. 2:13, Heb. 10:19
6. Reconciliation-Col. 1:20
7. Justification- Rm. 5:9
8. Sanctification- Heb.13:12
9. Conquest of Evil- Heb. 12:14, Rev. 12:11
10. Basis of the new covenant- Heb. 13:20

11. Lord's Supper -Mt. 26:26-27
12. Purifies and gives life
13. Ratifies our covenant agreement
14. Washes & Cleanses us from every unrighteousness
15. Quenches our thirst
16. Deliverer us from destruction/diseases
17. Speaks better things than the blood of Abel
18. The Mark

SPIRITUAL SIGNIFICANCE OF THE BREAD FROM HEAVEN

Bread is a universal commodity
Every country in the world has some form of bread
Bread is associated with life, health, nourishment and prosperity.
Hence, Bread from Heaven:
-1- Gives life/strength
-2- Nourishes the body, soul
-3- Makes one grow spiritually into maturity
-4- Fill hungry soul
-5- He is everlasting life giving food
-6- Gives clear vision

CONCLUSION

The bread in this context does not refer to the Lord's Supper rather, the bread is Jesus Himself.

It is not a loaf of bread that gives eternal life, but Jesus gives eternal life.

It is the teaching about Jesus which we must believe in order to be saved.
It states that
-1- He was sent from God the Father
-2- That he always did the Father's will
-3- That he represents the Father
-4- That he teaches what the Father wants to hear
-5- That this teaching includes the fact of Jesus Death, burial and resurrection.
-6- That this teaching includes the fact that those who believe will have eternal life.
-7- This is the teaching that we can feast on and eat to have eternal life

FINALLY

• If you have not given your life to Jesus.

• You stand outside of Christ-Starving for spiritual nourishment.

• Your soul will wither and die without the spiritual food it needs to live forever.

• Will you partake of that bread today.

• To do so you must heed God's plan for Man's Salvation.

PRAYER: Oh God feed me with the bread of life in Jesus Name.

LECTURE 9
PLEADING THE BLOOD OF JESUS

MEMORY VERSE: Colossians 1:14 "In whom we have redemption through His blood, even the forgiveness of sins".

TEXT: Hebrews 9:11-15; EPH 1:7

INTRODUCTION

Many Pentecostal believers know the song or chorus which says, There is power mighty in the blood (2x) There is power mighty, in the blood of Jesus Christ There is power mighty in the blood

One may ask, what is the spiritual implication of the blood of Jesus? Of what spiritual value has the blood of Jesus? When should we plead the blood of Jesus? And what are the basic spiritual requirements for pleading the blood of Jesus? These are some of the questions, among others, that we will respond to in tonight's Bible Study. Meanwhile, pleading means **"to ask earnestly; make an earnest appeal"**. Pleading the blood of Jesus in this instance refers to bringing the blood of Jesus to bear on a given situation or circumstance - - **because there is power in the blood of Jesus.**

A. The Spiritual Implications of the Blood of Christ

The Bible refers to the death of Christ as a **sacrifice.**

1. In Eph. 5:2, Paul describes it as "a fragrant offering and sacrifice to God".
2. In 1 Cor 5:7, he (Paul) writes, "For indeed Christ, our Passover, was **sacrificed** for us".
3. Numerous references to Christ's blood are also suggestive of a **sacrifice:**
   a. there was "expiation by **His blood"** (Rom. 3:25)
   b. "we are justified **by His blood"** (Rom. 5:9)
   c. "in Him we have redemption **through His blood"** (Eph. 1:7)
   d. we "have been brought near **in the blood of Christ"** (Eph. 2:13)
   e. he has reconciled to Himself all things "making peace by **the blood of His cross"** (Col. 1:20)

B. Infinite Value of the Precious Blood of Jesus

The place of the creature in the scale of life determines the value of the blood.

First comes the blood of animals **Second** of higher value is the blood of man, because it bears the image of God (Gen. 9:6)

Third, of special esteem in the sight of God is the blood of the innocent and of martyrs (Gen. 4:10; Matt. 23:35)

Fourth, and most precious of all is the blood of Christ (1 Pet. 1:19; Heb 9:12), of infinite value because united with Deity.

The death of Christ on the cross was a perfect sacrifice for mankind. Therefore His blood has the following **infinite value,** among others:

1. His blood provides forgiveness of sin (Heb 9:22)
2. His blood cleanses the sinner as well as the believer (Heb 9:22, 23)
3. His blood delivers from bondage and captivity
4. His blood cleanses the conscience (Heb 9:14; 13:12)
5. His blood provides boldness and access into God's presence (Heb 10:19)
6. His blood is a paid ransom - - price payment for our redemption
7. His blood provides deliverance from enslavement and power of sin
8. His blood translates believers from death to life (Col 1:13)
9. His blood releases from dominion of sin and its guilt (Eph 1:7)
10. His blood restores us to God's ownership and fellowship (Is 43:1; Rom 3:24)
11. His blood provides eternal inheritance (Heb 9:15)
12. The blood of Jesus is the foundation for Christianity
13. The blood of Jesus is the basis of the new covenant (Heb 9:20; 10:29)
14. The blood of Jesus secures our redemption (Heb 9:12)
15. The blood of Jesus ushers in a perfect sacrifice (Heb 10:14)
16. The blood of Jesus sanctifies (Heb 13:12)
17. The blood of Jesus was shed for many (Matt 26:28; Mk 14:24)
18. The blood of Jesus produces eternal life (Jn. 6:54)
19. The blood of Jesus justifies the sinner and the believer (Rom. 5:9)
20. The blood of Jesus brings us closer to God (Eph. 2:13)

THE POWER IN THE BLOOD OF JESUS

21. The blood of Jesus supplies peace (Col. 1:20)
22. The blood of Jesus provides victory over Satan (Rev. 12:1)
23. The blood of Jesus washes away sin (Rev. 1:5)

C. When Do We Plead the Blood of Jesus?

1. When you need revival in your spirit
2. When you feel dryness in your spiritual life
3. When you face danger
4. When you need healing for your physical ailment
5. When praying for the sick and the afflicted
6. When you need the blood to fight for you
7. When you want to pull down the stronghold of darkness
8. When you are being pursued by the enemy
9. When you are under attack by the household wickedness
10. When you desperately desiring divine intervention in your difficult situation
11. When you are facing stubborn enemies in your environment
12. When you are under witchcraft attacks
13. When you about to sleep
14. When embarking on a journey
15. When you are praying for the salvation of your loved ones
16. When you are passing through trials and temptation
17. When you are confronting dark powers and principalities
18. When you are facing powers stronger than you
19. When you need to overcome re-occurring temptation
20. You plead the blood over your food
21. You plead the blood of Jesus over your family members
22. You plead the blood of Jesus over your business
23. You plead the blood of Jesus over your marriage
24. You plead the blood of Jesus over your dream life
25. You plead the blood of Jesus over your office
26. You plead the blood of Jesus over your sick bed
27. You plead the blood of Jesus over your property

D. Basic Spiritual Requirements for Pleading the Blood of Jesus

1. You must be born again (from above) (Jn. 3 : 3)

2. You must be filled with the Holy Ghost (Eph. 5 :18)

3. You must die to self (Rom. 6 :13)

4. You must kill the flesh (Rom. 8: 5)

5. You must be broken (Gal. 2 : ·20)

6. You must maintain a daily walk of holiness with the Lord Jesus Christ (1 Pet. 1 : 16)

PRAYER POINTS

1. I plead the blood of Jesus over every situation in my life, in the name of Jesus

2. I plead the blood of Jesus over every dark powers of my father's house

3. Blood of Jesus arise, kill every sickness in my body.

CONCLUSION:

Since the blood of Christ is the foundation of Christianity, every believers in Christ has the authority to plead that blood at any situation or circumstance, for the blood of Christ has never loosen its power.

LECTURE 10
THE LORD'S SUPPER AND THE BLOOD OF JESUS

MEMORY VERSE"....To eat THE LORD'S SUPPER...the LORD JESUS.. when he had given thanks......took the cup.. saying, this cup is the new testament in MY BLOOD: this do ye...in remembrance of me. 1 Cor. 11:20, 24-25.

TEXT: Matt. 26:26-30; Mk. 14:22-26; 1 Cor. 11:23-34.

INTRODUCTION

The LORD'S supper is a symbolic meal which our Lord Jesus Christ established and commanded; in which Christians remember His sacrifice for our sins; the price that was paid on the cross for our redemption; and the acknowledgement of our sharing in the benefits of His death. The two elements for the LORD'S supper are "the unleavened bread" (Matt. 26:17,26) and "the fruit of the vine" (grape juice) - Mk. 14:25. The "bread" was broken, symbolizing the marred & striped body of Christ for our healing (Lk. 22:19; Isa. 53:4,5) and the "grape juice" - the cup, symbolized the BLOOD OF CHRIST shed for the remission of our sins (Lk. 22:20), so, all believers

(new creatures) are supposed to partake in it (1 Cor. 10:16, 17). The LORD'S supper is also called "the breaking of bread" (Acts 2:42; 20:7); the "Holy communion" (1 Cor. 10:16); and "the LORD'S Table" (1 Cor. 10:21). For a thorough understanding of the connection of the LORD'S supper and the Blood of Jesus, we must examine the following:

1. The Passover & the LORD'S Supper
2. The Purposes of the LORD's Supper
3. The Principles of the LORD'S Supper
4. The Perversion of the LORD'S Super
5. The Provisions in the LORD'S Supper
6. The precautions in the LORD'S Supper
7. The Penalties on the LORD'S Supper

THE PASSOVER & THE LORD'S SUPPER

Some important facts on the Passover & the Lord'S supper are:

1. Passover is an annual Celebration of the Jewish people (Ex. 12:14)

2. Passover is a reminder of the deliverance of the Jews from slavery in Egypt (Duet. 16:1-3; Ex.12:14)

3. Passover Lamb without blemish was killed in every household as commanded by God (Ex. 12:3-6)

4. Passover Lamb's blood was sprinkled on the two side posts and the upper doorpost (the lintel) of the house (Ex. 12:7)

5. Passover Lamb was then roasted with fire and was eaten with unleavened bread and with bitter herbs (Ex. 12:8-11)

6. Passover "blood" of the lamb shielded the Jews from the destructive plague and the Angel of death (Ex. 12:12-13, 23, 29-30)

7. Passover Lamb from God (Jesus) was identified by John the Baptist as the one that "taketh away the sin of the world (Jn. 1:29; 35-36)

8. Passover feast was celebrated by Jesus and His disciples in a large furnished "upper room" (Lk. 22:7-16)

9. Passover feast was replaced with the LORD'S Supper by Jesus in the same large furnished "upper room" (Lk. 22:14-20)

10. Passover Lamb that was "sacrificed for us" was Christ Jesus OUR LORD.(1 Cor. 5:7)

THE PURPOSES OF THE LORD'S SUPPER

1. To look "Backward" - To remember "His death" i.e. the Sacrifice of Christ at the cross of calvary; the price he paid for our redemption." This do in rememberance of me." (Lk. 22:19)

2. To look "Upward" - To bless God & offer thanksgiving to the most High for his "Sacrificed Lamb" without blemish. "He took the bread and gave thanks... And he took the cup, and gave thanks..".(Lk.22:19; Matt. 26:27)

3. To look "Inward". - To examine "self"; to confess all unconfessed sins and to amend our ways before God. (1 Jn. 1:9; Jer. 7:3-7) "Let a man examine himself, and so let him eat of that bread, and drink of that cup (1 Cor. 11:28)

4. To look "Around"- To see yourself and your fellow brethren as "one body" and "one bread" in Christ(1 Cor. 10:16,17) keeping the feast with them, "Not with "the leaven" of malice and wickedness; but with the "unleaven Bread" of sincerity and truth" (1 Cor. 5:8)

5. To look "Forward"- To expect the LORD'S return by keeping ourselves in the faith and dedicating our lives to do His WILL "showing forth the LORD'S death till he come" (1Cor. 11:26)

THE PRINCIPLES OF THE LORD'S SUPPER

There are 3 major principles on how to observe the LORD'S supper:

1. "ANY DAY" - The communion could be taken on any day of the week.
   (i) Every day - (Acts 2:46) " daily"
   (ii) Every week - (Acts 20:7) "weekly"
2. "ANY PLACE" - It could be taken in any place that believers gather.
   (i) In the church - (Act 2:41, 42; 1 Cor. 11:33)
   (ii) In private Homes - (Acts 2:46; Matt. 26:18, 26-30)
3. "ANY TIME"- It could be taken at any time; morning, noon or night
   (i) As often as ye drink it (1 Cor. 11:25)
   (ii) As often as ye eat it (1 Cor. 11:26)

THE PERVERSION OF THE LORD'S SUPPER

1. "Self-centered" instead of "Christ-centered"
   (a) "Self-Centered" - The gathering of brethren with selfish interest, and despising attitudes leading to division and strifes among brethren. (1Cor. 11:17-22)
   (b) "Christ-Centered" - We are to gather together to partake of the LORD'S SUPPER "in remembrance of him," so Christ must be the focus. (1 Cor. 11:24,25)
2. "Sacraments" instead of "Memorial"
   (a) Sacraments - This speaks of the performance of the LORD'S supper "TO OBTAIN GRACE"
   (b) Memorial - This speaks of the LORD'S Supper "In remembrance" of "THE OBTAINED GRACE"

THE PROVISIONS IN THE LORD'S SUPPER

As you partake of the Lord's supper in faith, certain impartation are expected through the Power in "His flesh" and "His Blood":

1. Power over sins & Bad Habits (Rom. 6:14; Heb. 9:22; Col. 1:13-14)
2. Freedom from spiritual imprisonment (Zech. 9:11,12)
3. Life impartation (resurrection power) (John 6: 53-55)
4. Power for "Divine Union" (His presence) (John 6:56)
5. Spiritual Blood Transfusion (Jn. 6:57)
6. Divine Revelational Knowledge (Lk. 24:30-31; Col. 1:9)
7. Dominion Over Death (Long Life Licence) (Jn. 6:58)
8. Mental Excellence (Spirit of understanding) (Lk. 24:30; Eph. 1:18)
9. Youthful Restoration (Health) (Ps. 103:5; Job 33:21-25)
10. Destruction of Poisons in your Body (2 Kings 4:38-41)

THE PRECAUTIONS IN THE LORD'S SUPPER

10 things to "watch" according to 1 Cor. 11:17-34

1. Be saved & Fit (repentance) for the feast (v. 28,31-32; 1 Jn. 1:9)
2. Have regard for the LORD (His Blood)- (V.27; 1 Sam. 2:30)
3. Have regard for His Church (His Body) - (V.22,29)
4. Have regard for the needies (v 22; Acts 2 :44; 45)
5. Avoid Divisions & Strife among Brethren (v. 18.34)
6. Avoid Drunkenness & surfeiting (v. 21; Lk. 21:34)
7. Avoid Heresies & stand by the truth (v. 19)
8. Avoid "Eating" & "Drinking" it "unworthily" (v.27, 29-30) (i.e partake with "faith in God" & "love for brethren")
9. Exercise faith for "His provisions" through "His Death (v. 26)
10. Exercise patience "one for another" (v. 33)

THE PENALTIES ON THE LORD'S SUPPER

There are penalties of damnation upon all partakers in an unworthy manner. Who are these kinds of partakers?

1. Those who despised the "precautions" above-1 Cor.11:17-34
2. Those who are living in open sins without amendments-1 Cor.5:1-5
3. Those "still" under church discipline for certain "unchristian conducts" (1 Cor. 5:9; 2 Thess. 3:6, 14-15)
4. Those who despised necessary restitutions (Lk. 19:8)
5. Those with unforgiving Spirits, walking in malice & bitterness among Brethren (Matt. 18:33-35, 15-17)
6. Those that have not been Baptized in water by immersion after their conversion (Acts 2:41-42)
7. Those engaging in secret sins & works of the flesh (Gal. 5:19-21)
- The penalties of damnation for such partakers (1 Cor. 11:30) are: 1. weakness 2. Sickness; and 3. death

CONCLUSION

These are Great "Blessings" & Great "Breakthroughs" for ALL "Believers" that thoroughly study this ordinance in order to partake and take advantage of "His provisions" for us - showing forth "The LORD'S Death till He come" (1 Cor. 11:26)

PRAYER POINT

Blood of Jesus, transfuse my blood, in the name of Jesus.

LECTURE 11
REDEMPTION BY THE BLOOD OF JESUS

MEMORY VERSE: In whom we have redemption through his blood, the forgiveness of sins, according to the riches of his grace; Eph 1:7.

This Scripture presents the blood of Jesus Christ as the infinite purchase price of our redemption. It also highlights two of the great conceptions of the Christian faith Redemption and Forgiveness.

TEXT: Rom 3:24 25, Heb 9:12-15, I Pet 1:18-23, Rev 5:9.
These Scriptures remind us of the following:
1. That the redemption we have in Christ is through His blood.
2. That the sacrificial death of Christ on the Cross is what procures the believers redemption.
3. That we were redeemed or bought back again by a ransom paid to God the Father.
4. That the purchase price for our redemption was not with corruptible things; but with the precious blood of the perfect Lamb of God.

5. That Christ gave His innocent blood to secure forgiveness and reconcile us with God.
6. That we are bought with the infinite purchase price that is equal to the purchase.

INTRODUCTION

The blood of Jesus is central to the New Testament concept of redemption and there are certain terms that are relative to this concept.
1. The word Redemption
2. The word Ransom
3. The Doctrine of Redemption
4. The Covenant of Redemption
5. The Cost of Redemption
6. The Scope of Redemption
7. The Perfect Redemption

REDEMPTION IN THE OLD AND NEW TESTAMENTS
In the Old Testament
As a means for balancing justice and setting matters straight, God designated various sacrifices and offerings to atone for or cover sins, including that of the priests and Levites.
1. In the Old Testament, Worshippers are expected to

present offerings which normally involve animal sacrifice.

2. Life of innocent animals will be taken.

3. Animals must be without blemish or defect.

4. Blood of animals were used as the price for the atonement of sin but cannot take away sin.

5. The High Priest usually makes atonement year by year continually, in the Holy of Holies of the earthly tabernacle for own sin and sins of the people.

6. Redemption was applied to properties, animals, persons and the nation of Israel.

7. The greatest Old Testament redemptive event is the Exodus From Egypt (Exodus 6-7)

1. **In the New Testament,** redemption refers to salvation from sin, death and wrath of God.

2. The New Testament teaching of redemption was foreshadowed by redemption in the Old Testament.

3. Jesus Christ was the ultimate substitute for mankind who gave His life to offer a perfect sacrifice once only and provide perfect Salvation.

4. New Testament redemption is eternal. Christ offered the true atonement with His own blood which brings eternal redemption

5. Jesus Christ the Heavenly High Priest who has an unchangeable priesthood made atonement once and once only, for the people, unlike the Earthly high priest.

GOD IS THE AUTHOR OF REDEMPTION

1. The need for redemption came about through the rebellion in Eden (Gen 3:1-7). From that account, seven principles are set forth.

2. God requires shedding of blood for sin to provide forgiveness (Heb 9:22)The covering provided (blood sacrifice) must be accepted.

3. The blood must be applied to have a protective covering. (Exo. 12:1 13)

4. The blood is necessary to provide sinners an acceptable covering for their sins. (Lev. 17:11)

THE POWER IN THE BLOOD OF JESUS

5. God provided the sacrifice, the ultimate sacrifice is called the Lamb of God (John 1:29)

6. The innocent must die for the guilty.

7. God brought judgment upon the sacrifice. Isa 53:4-7 clearly brings out this truth.

SIGNIFICANCE OF BLOOD OF JESUS TO REDEMPTION (I PETER 1:18-20)

Because of the power and efficacy in the blood of Jesus, it is called in the Scriptures by many descriptive names.1.

1. It is incorruptible blood (I Pet 1:18-19)
2. It is a Sinless blood
3. It is a precious blood (I Pet 1:18-19)
4. It is an innocent blood (I Pet 2: 22-24, Matt 27:4)
5. It is the blood of the perfect Lamb of God John 1:29, Rev 7:14
6. It is eternal blood (Heb 9:12)
7. It is an overcoming blood (Rev 12:11)

ACCOMPLISHMENTS OF REDEMPTION BY THE BLOOD OF JESUS

1. Redemption makes us to enjoy covenant of divine health Isa 53:5, 3 John 2) Divine health now becomes our heritage and birth right to be in God's priority for complete health. On the day that Christ died He did not only pay for our sins but also for our sickness.

2. Redemption makes us citizen of heaven and has established a spiritual status for us that give us the privilege to live a heavenly life here in this world. (Eph. 3: 20, 2:4-6)

3. We belong to the royalty (Rev. 5:9-10)

4. We have dominion (Psalm 82:6)

5. Redemption delivers us from:
- Sin (Matt. 1:21, I John 3:5)
- Law (Rom. 6:14)
- Power of the Devil (Col. 1: 13, 2:15, Heb. 2:14-15)
- God's wrath (Rom. 5:9, I Thess. 1:10)
- Eternal death (John. 3:16-17)
- Present Evil world (Gal. 1:4, 2 Pet. 2:11)

CONCLUSION

The greatest and highest price that can be acceptable to God as atonement is the blood of Jesus, because of its eternal merit and efficacy. It is the only incorruptible, eternal, divine, sinless, perfect, overcoming, precious blood of the perfect Lamb of God, Jesus Christ that satisfied God's demand for our redemption.

PRAYER POINT

1. Redemption in the Blood of Jesus, deliver me from the bondage and slavery of sin, in the name of Jesus.

LECTURE 12
THE BLOOD OF THE LAMB

MEMORY VERSE:

John 1 v 29 The next day John seeth Jesus coming unto him, and saith, Behold the Lamb of God, which taketh away the sin of the world.

TEXTS: Heb. 9:22; Zach. 9:11-12; I Pet. 1:19

INTRODUCTION

The theme of the entire bible is "The Lamb of God". He is pictured typically in Israel's sacrifices, but He is revealed in the New Testament as Jesus Christ, the Son of God- the lamb of God, who died that we might live.

He bore our sins on Calvary and shed His blood to put away our sins once and for all. The blood of the Lamb is also referred to as 'the blood of the passover', the sprinkling blood, and the blood of the covenant.'

REQUIREMENTS OF LAMB SACRIFICE AND OUR LORD JESUS CHRIST.

1. The Lamb must be perfect (without spot or blemish) Exo. 12 v5; Lev. 23 v 12; Lev. 22 v 20, 1 Peter1:19
2. The Lamb was to be a sin offering: Lev. 4 v 32; I John 2 v 2
3. The Lamb had to be slain: Lev 14 v 12-13; Isa 53 v 8; Rev 5 v 11-12
4. A Lamb for the whole race.

In the Old Testament i.e. in Genesis 4 v 4, Lev 14 v 11-14, there was a Lamb offered for a man. In Exodus, the Passover pictures a Lamb for a house(family) Exo 12 v 3 and in Levitucus, a Lamb was offered for the nation of Israel – Lev. 16 v 19-34; 23 v 26-32; Heb. 9 v 7, 25

THE NEED FOR A SUPERIOR SACRIFICE

According to the scriptures, The old testament sacrifices were defective for the following reasons:
1) They did not provide the true remission of sin,
2) They did not make the worshippers perfect, Heb 10
3) Every year there was the constant reminder of sins- Heb.10:3. In addition to the daily and monthly sacrifices, there were the annual sacrifices on the Day of Atonement, which reminded them their sins and need for cleansing.
4) It was not possible for the blood of bulls and goats to take away sins. Heb.10:4

However, the sacrifices of the old covenant, accomplished some purposes by serving as a shadow of the good things to come, which are:
- His better sacrifice
- The better Hope
- The eternal redemption and the eternal inheritance.

Hence, the superior sacrifice which was
1) Provided by God , Heb. 10:5-6
2) Offered freely by Christ. John 6:38
3) Established a new covenant – Heb. 9:15.

SUBSTITUTIONARY DEATH – THE GREAT EXCHANGE

1 Peter 3:18 'For Christ also suffered once for sins, the just for the unjust, that He might bring us to God, being put to death in the flesh, but Quickened by the Spirit.'
Matthew 20:28. 'Even as the Son of man came not to be ministered unto, but to minister, and to give His life a ransom for many.'
The death of Christ is to make reconciliation for the sins of the people, and translate us as follows:
➢ From the Kingdom of darkness into the Kingdom of Light.
➢ Sinners to saints
➢ Unrighteous to righteous
➢ Death to Living Souls
➢ Poverty to Riches
➢ Failure to Success
➢ Accursed to Blessed
➢ Sickness to Divine Health.

CHARACTERISTICS OF THE BLOOD OF THE LAMB

The Blood that flowed in Jesus' body which made Him a perfect sacrifice was;
* Pure blood – Acts 20:28
* holy blood- 1 Peter 1:18-19
* Innocent blood
* living blood
* Incorruptible blood and
* Precious (rare) blood.

DESCRIPTION OF THE BLOOD (NATURE AND WORK OF THE BLOOD)

1. Justifying – Rom 5 v 9
2. Redeeming – Rev 5 v 9
3. Remitting – Heb 9 v 22
4. Forgiving – Eph 1 v 7
5. Washing and freeing – Rev 1 v 5
6. Purging – Heb 9 v 14
7. Cleansing – I John 1 v 7
8. Sanctifying – Heb. 13 v 12
9. Reconciling – Eph 2 v 13
10. Blotting – Col 2 v 14
11. Triumphing – Col 2 v 15
12. Overcoming Rev 12 v 11
13. Agreeing – I John 5 v 8

14. Communing – I Cor 10 v 16
15. Purchasing – Acts 20 v 28
16. Sprinkling – Heb 12 v 24
17. Speaking – Heb 12 v 24
18. Incorruptible – I Pet 1 v 19
19. Precious – I Pet 1 v 19
20. Holy – Heb 10 v 29
21. Atoning – Lev 17 v 11
22. Innocent – Matt 27 v 14
23. Accessing – Heb 10 v 19
24. Perfect – John 19 v 30
25. Sheltering – Exo 12 v 23
26. Shed – Luke 22 v 20
27. Saving – Zech 9 v 11
28. Whitening – Rev 7 v 14-15
29. Peacemaking – Col 1 v 2

THE POWER IN THE BLOOD OF THE LAMB- I PET 1 V 18-19

1. It redeems – Col 1v 12-15
2. It blots out sins – Heb 9 v 13-14
3. It brings us into fellowship WITH God – Eph 2 v 12-13; Heb 10 v 19-21
4. It makes peace – Col 1 v 20
5. It justifies – Rom 5 v 8-9; Rom 8 v 1
6. It cleanses – I John 1 v 7
7. It removes and breaks curses. Gal.3:13

8. It provides for our healing and keeps us in divine health.
9. It gives victory over sin, Satan and the works of darkness
10. It provides a New and Better Covenant

WHAT TO DO WITH THE BLOOD?

1) Accept the blood by faith
2) Appropriate the blood
3) Plead the blood
4) Apply the blood to your circumstances
5) Share the Lamb of God with friends
6) Stay under the cover of the blood.

CONCLUSION: So what animal sacrifices could not accomplish, God did by the sending of His Son who freely accepted the task of offering Himself for sin, keeping with the will of God, providing what the Law could not. Jesus Christ is the Lamb Of God. So perfectly perfect and completely complete is His offering of Himself that He could say of His work, 'It is finished' (John 19:30). Therefore, there is no further need for more blood sacrifices. Heb. 10:12

PRAYER POINTS

1) I cover my destiny with the blood of Jesus
2) My father, sanitize my life with the blood of Jesus
3) I release the arsenal of the blood to the camp of the enemy, in the Name of Jesus.

LECTURE 13
SANCTIFICATION THROUGH THE BLOOD OF JESUS

MEMORY VERSE: "And such were some of you: but ye are washed, but ye are sanctified, but ye are justified in the name of the Lord Jesus, and by the Spirit of our God." 1 Cor 6:11.

TEXTS: 1 Cor. 6:9-11; Jer. 1:4-5; Heb. 13:8-12; Heb. 9:11-15.

INTRODUCTION

God desires His people to obey Him, to hate sin and love righteousness (Isa. 5:16). God Himself set aside people or things for divine use, they are consecrated or made sacred. They are washed in the blood of the lamb sanctified and justified in the name of the Lord. The blood of Jesus is of great importance for sanctification. It purifies, cleanses, consecrate, justify (Rom. 5:9), redeem (Rom. 3:24) reconcile, sufficient, ensures and gives new life.

WHAT IS SANCTIFICATION?
1. Is to be separated and endowed with great power (Job. 5:1; Dan. 8:13)
2. Is to be set aside for use by God (Isa. 35:8)
3. Is to be growing in holiness (Jer. 23:9)
4. Is to be consecrated or made sacred (Ps. 16:3)

FACTS TO NOTE ABOUT SANCTIFICATION BY THE BLOOD OF JESUS
1. Jesus Christ is our sanctification (1 Cor. 1:30)
2. Sanctification is brought about by the spirit when one is made a new creature (1 Peter 1:2)
3. In sanctification both the person being sanctified and what is being used to sanctify must be clean and spotless.
4. The blood of Jesus has a cleansing power (Exo. 29:21)
5. Sanctification is part of salvation and its received with salvation (2 Tim. 3:13)
6. Sanctification can be obtained through the atonement of the blood of Jesus Christ (Heb. 10:10; 13:12)
7. Sanctification can be described as separation to the services of God (Ps. 4:3; 2 Cor. 6:17).
8. None can inherit the kingdom of God without sanctification (1 Cor. 6:9-11)
9. Sanctification is not limited to human beings (Lev. 27:14-33)

SANCTIFICATION CAN BE BROUGHT ABOUT BY

1. God (Ezek. 37:28; Jude 1)
2. Christ (Heb. 2:11)
3. The Holy Spirit (Rom. 15:16; 1 Peter 1:2)
4. Truth (John 17:17)
5. The blood of Jesus Christ (Heb. 9:14)
6. Prayer (1 Tim. 4:4-5)
7. By faith (Acts 26:18)
8. The blood of the covenant (Heb. 10:29)
9. The name of Jesus (1 Cor. 6:11)
10. The word of God (John 15:3)

SANCTIFICATION AND THE BLOOD OF JESUS

1. When you are made righteous by the blood of Jesus (1 Cor. 1:30)
2. When you become dead to sin (Rom. 6)
3. When elected by the blood of Jesus (Eph. 1:4)
4. When washed from sin by the blood of the blood of Jesus (1 Cor. 6:11)
5. When justified by the blood of Jesus (Rev. 1:5)
6. When one is cleansed by the blood of Jesus (Heb. 10:29)
7. When redeemed by the blood of Jesus (Luke 1:66-67)
8. When saved by the blood of Jesus (1 Thess. 4:3-4)
9. When purified by the blood of Jesus (Acts 11:14-18)
10. When purged by the blood of Jesus (2 Peter 1:4-10)
11. When reconciled to God by the blood of Jesus (2 Cor. 5:17-21)
12. When converted and your sin blotted out by the blood of Jesus (Acts 3:19-21)
13. When purchased by the blood of Jesus (Acts 20:28)
14. When you become perfect by the blood of Jesus (John 19:30)
15. When you triumph and overcome by the blood of Jesus (Rev. 12:11)

THINGS THAT CAN BE SANCTIFIED

1. The people (Exo. 31:13)
2. The congregation (Joel 2:18)
3. The first born (Exo. 13:2)
4. Your first fruit offering (Rom. 15:16)
5. The altar (Exo. 29:36)
6. The day (Gen. 2:3)
7. The temple/tabernacle (2 Chron. 7:16)

8. Fasting (Joel 2:15)
9. House (Lev. 27:14)
10. Bread (1 Sam. 21:5)
11. Field (Lev. 27:16)
12. Vessels (2 Chro. 29:29)
13. Gates (Neh. 3:1)
14. Your heart (1 Peter 3:15)
15. Yourself (Lev. 20:7)
16. The Lord of Host (Isa. 8:13)

WHAT TO DO

1. Be born again (1 John 2:29)
2. Put off the old man (Eph. 4:22-24)
3. Become dead to sin and run to God for forgiveness (Acts 26:13)
4. Accept Christ as the offering for sin (1 Cor. 1:30)
5. Let your Spirit be renewed (Titus 3:5)
6. Become the temple of God (Rom. 8:9)
7. Be baptised into Christ by the Spirit (Gal. 3:27)

CONCLUSION: The blood of the lamb is the sure sanctification and remission for our sin. It destroys evil covenant and gives a new name that reflects the glory of God. The blood of Jesus is the only one that can purify and make you whole.

PRAYER POINT

1. Blood of Jesus, deliver my foundation and set me free, in the name of Jesus.

2. I receive divine sanctification by the power in the blood of Jesus.

LECTURE 14
PROTECTION THROUGH THE BLOOD OF JESUS

Hymn: Christ our Redeemer died
on the cross
Died for the sinner paid all
his due
Sprinkle your soul with the
blood of the Lamb
And I will pass, will pass
over you.

Chorus: When I see the blood
When I see the blood
When I see the blood
I will pass, I will pass over you.

MEMORY VERSE:

"And the blood shall be to you for a token upon the houses where ye are: and when I see the blood, I will pass over you, and the plague shall not be upon you to destroy you, when I smite the land of Egypt." Ex 12:13

TEXTS: Ex. 12:1-14; Rev. 12:10-11; Matt. 26:26-28; Mk. 14:22-24; 1 Cor. 11:23-26; Mk. 16:17-18; Ps. 61:1-3; Ps. 18:10; Phil. 2:9-11; Lk. 10:19; Isa. 43:1-3; Ps. 91; Ps. 27:1-6; Isa. 49:24-26; Jer. 20:9-12; Ps. 34:18-22; Acts 27:14-44; Acts 28:1-10.

INTRODUCTION

To protect means to defend, care for, guard, keep safe, look after, mount guard over, preserve, safeguard, save, secure, shelter, shield, watch over, to take under one's wing, covers, cover up for, save from harm. This is exactly what the blood of Jesus Christ does for every true child of God. As a hen covers her chicks, that is how the blood of Jesus Christ covers the children of God. The original purpose of the blood of Jesus Christ is to pay for the sins of mankind and continue protecting the saved souls till they get to heaven. This blood of Jesus Christ is of immeasurable value to God and to man (1 Peter ..:18-19). This blood shields the believer from all evil. By virtue of the power of this blood, the believer constantly hides under the shadow of the Almighty (Ps. 19:1). That is why a popular Christian gospel song says; "I'm gonna stay right under the blood (of Jesus), and the devil can do me no harm."

SPIRITUAL SIGNIFICANCE OF BLOOD

1. Blood is life, for life is in it.
2. When blood is split, life goes out.

3. The law of vengeance calls that blood must be shed for blood.
4. Sin is the transgression of God's law.
5. Sin is disobedience to God.
6. Disobedience to God attracts death.
7. When death is administered to the disobedient, God's demand for justice has been met.
8. When blood is shed, the voice crying for vengeance is silenced.
9. Blood sacrifice was necessitated by the fall of man in the Garden of Eden.
10. Only sinless blood could ever redeem man from depravity.

THE HEATHENIC USE OF BLOOD

1. The heathens do all kinds of strange things with blood
2. The sacrifice blood of animals, birds, reptiles, and even human beings
3. They drink blood
4. They sprinkle blood
5. They apply blood
6. They do all of the above to:
- ward off evil
- appease demons or spirits
- pay debts they owe spirits
- invoke evil on others
- invoke vengeance on others
- silence the cry of ancestral powers
- acquire greater evil powers
- fulfil tradition and customs.

OLD TESTAMENT USE OF BLOOD

1. The God of Israel required blood sacrifice.
2. The blood of the following were used in sacrifice to Him:
- birds
- goats
- sheep
- bulls
3. Unclean creatures were never sacrificed to God
4. God determined the pattern for such sacrifices
5. Special persons (priests) were consecrated to perform this function
6. The old testament blood sacrifices never washed away sins
7. They only covers sins
8. They only appeased God's anger against man's sins temporarily, waiting for the Perfect Sacrifice (Jesus Christ) to come.

THE PERFECT SACRIFICE – THE BLOOD OF JESUS CHRIST

1. God personally prepared Jesus Christ to come into this world to shed His holy blood for all of mankind
2. Jesus Christ is the perfect sacrifice
3. His blood is the perfect blood
4. His blood is sinless
5. His blood is eternally powerful
6. Every other power bows to His blood
7. The blood of Jesus Christ brought the atonement i.e. "At-one-moment."
8. His blood paid for all the sins of mankind
9. His blood satisfied God
10. His blood made God to smile at mankind once more
11. His blood did not just cover the sins of man
12. His blood actually WASHED AWAY the sins of man forever
13. Herein lies the secret of the PROTECTIVE POWER in the blood of Jesus.

PROTECTION-APPLICATION OF THE BLOOD OF JESUS

1. Every child of God is entitled to be protected by the blood of Jesus Christ.
2. The kingdom of darkness fears, dreads and respects this blood
3. You must know your RIGHT to use this blood
4. You must know HOW to use this blood
5. You must go ahead and begin to use this blood
6. You must use it by faith and boldly too.
7. This blood silences every voice of accusation from the kingdom of darkness.
8. It pleads for mercy for the saints before God continually.
9. It washes away all sins
10. It heals all sicknesses
11. It silences all enemies and avengers
12. Apply this blood to your spirit, soul and body always
13. Apply it to your health
14. Apply it to your business
15. Apply it to your marriage
16. Apply it to your foundation
17. Apply it to your relationships

18. Apply it to the call of God on your life
19. Apply it to your ministry and finance
20. Apply it to your properties and belonging
21. Apply it to your national and inter-national affairs

THE BLOOD OF JESUS AS THE NOTE OF FINAL VICTORY

1. The blood of Jesus Christ qualifies you to go to heaven
2. It sanctifies and purifies you to be heaven-worthy
3. It makes the angels happy to WALK and WORK with you
4. It gives you a SECOND CHANCE with God
5. It gives you many extra chances with God – so long as you are still alive on earth.
6. It makes you RAPTURABLE
7. It ensures your ULTIMATE VICTORY in life and eternity

CONCLUSION: It will help you tremendously to cultivate the holy habit of making full use of the blood of Jesus Christ. Drink it, rub it, sprinkle it, apply it, plead it, respect it, honour it, circle everything about and yours with it, soak your whole being in the ocean of the blood of Jesus Christ always. Sing about the power in that blood always. Then, trust God to perfect all that concerns you and all yours now and forever!

Song to Sing:

1. What can wash away my sins?
2. Oh! The blood of Jesus...
3. I am delivered, praise the Lord...

PRAYER:
Blood of Jesus Christ, appear, fight for me, in the name of Jesus.

LECTURE 15
RECONCILIATION THROUGH THE BLOOD OF JESUS

MEMORY VERSE: And that he might reconcile both unto God in one body by the cross, having slain the enmity thereby. Eph. 2:16

TEXTS: Col. 1:20-21; 2 Cor. 5:17-20

INTRODUCTION

The blood is a red fluid that is pumped from the heart and circulates around the bodies of humans. It seems to be the most important element in the body without which none can live (Lev. 17:11). Reconciliation means ending of conflict or renewing a friendly relationship between disputing people or groups. It is making of two or more apparently conflicting things consistent or compatible. Confession and repentance that makes sinners forgiven and acceptable to God.

FACTS ABOUT BLOOD
1. Without blood we cannot live (Lev. 17:11).
2. Only animals that don't make sound have no blood e.g worms.
3. There is no substitute for blood in human body.
4. God says we must not eat blood (Gen. 9:4; Lev. 3:17).
5. God says we must not shed blood (Deut. 5:17).
6. Anyone who sheds blood must have his own bloodshed.
7. Blood diseases often lead to terminal death.
8. Shedding of animal blood does not constitute sin.
9. When you shed blood both you and your children will pay for it.
10. Any animal shedding human blood must die.
11. Blood of Jesus is incorruptible.
12. Blood of Jesus is invisible.

HOW BLOOD GET OUT OF HUMAN BODY
1. Through accidents
2. Suicide
3. Murder
4. Man slaughter
5. Arson
6. Abortion
7. Battle, fight, war
8. Death sentence
9. Witchcraft activities
10. Careless-injury – biting fingers
11. Incision
12. Circumcision
13. Hospital operation
14. Child birth
15. Sacrifices

16. Occultic activities
17. Blood donation
18. Demonic barbers
19. Rituals
20. Kidnapping
21. Herbalist activities
22. Mercy killing
23. Body scratching
24. Pedicure/manicure
25. Long kissing
26. Doctor's injection
27. Disvirgin

MYSTERIES ABOUT BLOOD OF JESUS

1. Jesus was slain before the foundation of the world (Rev. 13:8).
2. Blood was used to atone for sin of Adam and Eve.
3. Blood is important as sacrifice
- Isaac connection (Heb. 11:17-19).
4. Blood was important in the Passover connection (Exo. 12:12-13).
5. Blood of Jesus had no contact with any other blood.
6. There was no contamination/pollution in the Blood of Jesus.
7. Jesus never experienced any sickness or diseases.

HOW JESUS BLOOD WAS SHED

1. During the last supper (Matt. 26:27-28).
2. At the garden of Gethsemane (Lk. 22:44).
3. When beaten with whip that had blades (1 Pet. 2:24).
4. When given crown of thorns (John. 19:2).
5. When His legs were nailed (John.19:37).
6. When His hands was nailed (John. 20:25-27).
7. When spear was thrust into Him (John. 19:34).

WHY DO WE NEED RECONCILIATION

1. Adam and Eve sinned against God.
2. We all have sinned (Rom. 3:13; 1 John. 1:8-9; Heb. 2:17).
3. Without forgiveness of sin, problems in this world.
4. Without forgiveness of sin no salvation.
5. Without forgiveness of sin all will go to hell fire.

RECONCILIATIONS IN THE BIBLE

1. Reconciliation on the alter with blood (Lev. 8:15)
2. Priests making reconciliation on the altar (2 Chro. 29:24).
3. Reconciliation for the peace of Israel (Ezek. 45:15).
4. Offering for reconciliation for house of Israel (Ezek. 45:17).
5. Making reconciliation for iniquities (Dan. 9:24).
6. The giving of the ministry of reconciliation (Matt. 5:18).
7. Commitment unto the word of reconciliation (Matt. 5:19; 2 Cor. 5:19).
8. Making reconciliation for the sins of the people (Heb. 2:17).

PRAYER POINTS

1. Anything in me driving God away from me be removed by fire in Jesus name.

2. Blood of Jesus blot out my sins, in the name of Jesus.

3. I refuse to go to hell by the power, in the blood of Jesus

CONCLUSION:

It is absolutely important for us all to be reconciled with Jesus if want to live in Jesus and reign with him.

LECTURE 16
VICTORY THROUGH THE BLOOD OF JESUS

Text: Heb 9: 11-15; Rev. 12: 5-12

Memory Verse: "And they overcame him by the blood of the Lamb and by the word of their testimony, and they loved not their lives unto the death" – Rev 12:11

(A) INTRODUCTION

For thousands of years, there has been a mighty conflict for the possession of mankind. Mighty conflict between the Old Serpent, who led man astray and "The Seed of the woman"

In our lives and in the lives of others, many times we could see the demonstration of the power of God and at other times, it would appear as if the devil is winning the battle. That has been the conflict between the power of darkness and the Kingdom of Light of our Lord Jesus Christ. But our God is a man war. He has never lost any battle.

(B) Some facts about our adversary, the devil

1. The devil, the great enemy of mankind once occupied a high position in heaven. He was an anointed cherub that covereth. He was once upon the holy mountain of God until iniquity was found in him – His heart was lifted up because of his beauty and he was sent packing from heaven. He was driven out of heaven – Isa 14:12; Eze 28:14; Rev 12: 7-9.

2. While heaven was rejoicing because the devil was sent packing from there, woe was declared to the inhabitants of earth – Rev. 12:12

3. On arrival at earth, he became the greatest enemy of mankind. He caused the first man Adam to disobey God which led to Adam to be driven out of the Garden of Eden. Man was driven out of the garden and from the presence of God the Almighty – Gen. 3: 23-24

4. By deceiving Adam, God cursed Adam, sin entered into the world, tragedies, calamites, sicknesses and diseases including death came as a result.

5. The devil our adversary is always walking about seeking whom to devour – 1 Peter 5:8. He is out there to steal and to kill and to destroy.

6. He went to God to obtain permission to tempt the servant of God - Job. Job 2:1-6
7. He withstood Joshua the High Priest, standing before the angel of the Lord resisting Joshua the High Priest until the Lord spoke to Satan: :The LORD rebuke thee O Satan, even the LORD that hath chosen Jerusalem rebuke thee; is not this a brand plucked out of the fire? And the Lord commanded that the filthy garment Joshua was wearing be removed - Zech 3: 1-2.

In all of these, the Bible says we overcame him by the blood of the Lamb.

(C) The Agonies Jesus Christ went through to obtain for us this precious victory over the devil

1. The agony of soul - Matt 26:38
2. He was betrayed - Lk 22:3
3. He was mocked - Lk 22:: 63
4. Falsely condemned to death - Mark 15:13
5. He was cruelly scourged - Matt 27: 26

6. He was ridiculed and abused - Matt 27: 29-31
7. Finally crucified - John 19:17 - 18

Beloved, Jesus Christ volunteered His body, mind and spirit to the suffering of the cross and the shedding of His blood for us to have victory in every area of our lives.

They overcame him by the Blood of the Lamp are the words of the song of victory. What a glorious victory for you and I.

Blood is a living thing and the Blood of Jesus Christ has the power to overcome anything that confronts you.

(D) What are these victories we have through the Blood of Jesus?

1. The victory of salvation through the blood of Jesus - Rom 5:9.

Salvation is the first victory handed over to us by the Blood of Jesus Christ.

2. The victory of redemption through the blood of Jesus – Eph 1:7; Rom 6:6
Since the fall of man, every one had been placed under God's curse which include poverty, sickness, torment and death. But thanks be to God for Jesus Christ has given us victory and right to freedom over these curses through His precious Blood.

3. The victory of atonement through the blood of Jesus – Rom 5:11

4. The victory of forgiveness through the blood of Jesus – Eph 1:7
When we confess our sins and ask for forgiveness, the Blood of Jesus removes them totally.

5. The victory of justification through the blood of Jesus – Rom 5: 8-11

But God demonstrates His own love towards us in that while we were still sinners Christ died for us. Much more than having now been justified by His Blood, we shall be saved from wrath through Him.

6. The victory of restoration – Eph 2: 13-14, 16

In the time of Christ, Gentiles were excluded from the family of God because they were part of the old covenant. They were aliens from the Commonwealth of Israel and strangers from the covenant of promise, having no hope and without God in the world.

But through the Blood of Christ, these two groups – the Jews and the Gentiles were made one.

7. Victory of being our mediator through the blood of Jesus – Heb 7:25

The Bible says "Wherefore he is able to also save them to the uttermost that come to God by Him seeing He ever liveth to make intercession for them.

8. Victory over the accuser – The Blood of Jesus enables us to overcome the power of our accuser, Satan.

9. The victory of cleansing through the blood of Jesus - 1 John 1:7
   The blood of Jesus Christ cleanses from all sin.

10. The victory of deliverance through the Blood of Jesus - Rev 12:11

11. The victory of healing through the Blood of Jesus - Isa 53: 5; 1 Peter 2:24

12. The victory of divine protection through the Blood of Jesus - Ex 12:13

13. Through the Blood of Jesus we have victory over sin and temptation - Heb 9:14

14. Through the Blood of Jesus we have peace with God - Col 1:20

(E) How to claim and maintain the victory

1. You must apply the blood to your heart by surrendering your life to Jesus and be born again.

2. You must believe that the victory over Satan and all his authority is by Blood of the Lamb.

3. You must realize that there can be no victory without conflict

4. You must be ready to fight spiritual warfare. The believer who desires to share in the victory over Satan through the Blood of Jesus must be a fighter.

5. You must live always under the holy consciousness that we are being watched every moment by an enemy of unimaginable cunning and power. Therefore you need to watch and pray.

6. You must realize that this strife is not against flesh and blood but against principalities, against powers, against the rulers of darkness of this world and against spiritual wickedness in high places - Eph 6:12

7. You must devote yourself in every way and at all costs to fight against all the works of flesh, the lust of eyes and the pride of life - 1 John 2:16

8. Have an aggressive faith because this is the victory that overcometh the world even our faith.

9. Always bring yourself and family daily under the cover of the pool of the Blood of Jesus. The Blood of the Sprinkling.

CONCLUSION

Beloved, I beseech all of you to open your entire being to the incoming power of the Blood of Jesus, then your life will become a continual demonstration of the power of resurrection and ascension of our Lord Jesus.

Prayers

1. Blood of Jesus, deliver me by fire in the name of Jesus

2. By the Blood of Jesus, every owner of evil load in my life, carry your load in the name of Jesus

3. Blood of Jesus, pursue poverty out of my life

LECTURE 17
HEALING BY THE BLOOD OF JESUS

MEMORY VERSE(S) *"In whom we have redemption through HIS BLOOD, even the forgiveness of sins.....who forgiveth all thine iniquities, who HEALETH all thy diseases. Col. 1:14; Psalm 103:3*

TEXT(S) Isa. 53:4-5; Matt. 8:16-17; 1 Pet. 2:24

INTRODUCTION

The Almighty God declared to His people that "I AM THE LORD THAT HEALETH THEE" (Ex. 15:26). This is a statement of fact on what Jesus Christ has accomplished through "HIS BLOOD" in our redemption package. "Healing" is included in salvation; for that word - Salvation means "deliverance", "healing", "preservation", "soundness", "Health" & "Wholeness" of Spirit, Soul & Body. As a redemptive Blessing in Christ, HEALING is a definite act of God through faith in Jesus by the power of the Holy Spirit, the word of God, and the precious BLOOD of Christ through which the Human body is cured, repaired, delivered from sickness and its power, and made as whole, sound and healthy as it was before the affliction. The Human race has been subjected to the problem of sickness and diseases due to the fall of man, sin, the execution of the law of sowing & reaping and the work of Satan & demons - But HEALING for All is in the atonement . When SIN is atoned for, naturally, the results of sin are likewise atoned for. No perfect remedy has ever been found that can cure diseases outside of the BLOOD of Jesus Christ. That Blood was shed from "HIS STRIPES". By these Stripes or wounds (from the whipping) we are Healed, so our Great physician has offered us TOTAL HEALTH Spiritually, mentally and physically as shown below:

- Healing of the Spirit (Translation)
- Healing of the Soul (Transformation)
- Healing of the Body (Transposition)

For a thorough understanding of this topic on "Healing by the Blood of Jesus", we'll need to look at the following sub-topics:

1. His Healing and His Atonement
2. His Healing and His Assurance
3. His Healing and His Abilities
4. His Healing and His Avenues
5. His Healing and All Afflictions

HIS HEALING AND HIS ATONEMENT- Lev. 17:11; Jn. 1:29; Eph. 1:7; Heb. 9:22; 1Jn.1:7; 1 Pet. 2:24

1. Healing is wrapped up in "the covenant" which was ratified in "His BLOOD" so, healing benefits are in the Atonement (Ex.15:26;24:5-8).
2. Healing is a part of "salvation", which was given on the basis of Atonement. "salvation" means - Healing,Health, soundness, preservation & deliverance (Rom. 1:16; Acts 3:16; 4:8-12)
3. Healing came to the Israelites in the wilderness by beholding the "brazen serpent" upon a pole. Beholding Christ on the cross gives healing through His Atonement (Num. 21:7-9;John. 3:14)
4. Healings by "the Stripes" of Jesus were made possible through "His sufferings" at the time of His Atonement for all men (Isa. 53:5; 1 Pet.2:24)
5. Healing is expected to accompany "conversion" and "redemption" by the Atonement (Isa. 6:10; Matt. 9:5-7; 13:14-16)

6. Healing from God is by a "RANSOM" which is another Hebrew word for Atonement. (Job 33:24) see verses 14-30
7. Healing through "HIS WORD" is made possible by the Atonement, because "the spirit" (Holy Spirit), "the water" (God's Word) and "THE BLOOD": these 3 agree in ONE. (Ps. 107:20; 1Jn.5:8)
8. Healing through spiritual transactions has been provided ONLY on the basis of Atonement. (Heb. 9:11-22; Jas. 5:14-16)
9. Healings in the ministry of Jesus , sometimes, were followed with "instructions" to "go & show yourself to the priests" to make the Atonement (Matt. 8:2-4; Lk.5;12-14; Lev.14:1-20)
10. Healing is needed to remove "sicknesses', which came as a result of "SIN" whose Only remedy is in the Atonement of Jesus Christ. (Matt. 8:16-17; Jn 1:29)
11. Healing of ALL "sicknesses" is to "destroy the works of the devil" which was in the mission of Jesus through His

Atonement. (1Jn. 3:8; Job 2:6-7; Acts 10:38)

12. Healing manifestations through the "gifts of the Holy Spirit" are the continuation of the works of Christ based on the "finished" work of His Atonement. (1Cor. 12:3-10; Heb 2:3-4)

HIS HEALING AND HIS ASSURANCE -Num.23:19; 2Cor. 1:20; Mal.3:6; Heb 13:8; Matt.24:35; Ps.119:89

1. Ex. 15:26 -"...I' am the LORD that HEALETH thee".
2. Jer. 30:17- "I will restore HEALTH to thee, and I will HEAL thee.."
3. Isa. 53:5 - "he was wounded....& with His stripes we are HEALED.
4. Ps. 103:3 - "..(the LORD) HEALETH all thy diseases."
5. Deut.7:15 - "And the Lord will take away from thee ALL sickness.."
6. Matt. 10:1-"He gave them POWER..to HEAL all sicknesses.
7. Matt. 8:16 -"...He HEALED all that were sick.

8. Ps. 107:20 -"He sent HIS WORD, and HEALED them..."
9. Acts. 9:34 -"..Jesus Christ maketh thee Whole....."
10. Matt.8:17-"..Himself took our infirmities & BARE our sicknesses."
11. Ps.30:2 - "O LORD, I cried unto thee, & thou hast HEALED me."
12. Mal.4:2 - "But unto you...shall the SUN of righteousness arise with HEALING in his wings..."

HIS HEALING AND HIS ABILITIES -Matt. 19:26; Mk. 9:23; Lk.1:37

1) His Abilities to Heal afflictions from Birth
- The Blind from Birth - Jn. 9:1-7
- The Cripple from Birth - Acts 14:8-10
- The Lame from Birth - Acts 3:2-8
2) His Abilities to Heal afflictions of many years
- 12 years issue of Blood - Mk 5:25-29
- 18 years demonic infirmity- Lk. 13:11-13
- 38 years infirmity of impotence - Jn. 5:5-9
3) His Abilities to Heal afflictions at the point of death
- Centurion's Servant - Luke 7:2-10
- Epaphroditus - Phil. 2:25-27

- King Hezekiah - Isa. 38:1-5
4) His Abilities to raise even those afflicted unto death
- Son of the widow at Zarephath - 1Kings 17:17-23
- Son of the Shunammite woman - 2Kings 4:32-37
- Son of the widow at Nain City - Lk. 7:11-15
- Daughter of ruler at Synagogue - Lk. 8:49-55
- Lazarus of Bethany - John. 11:39-44
- Tabitha (Dorcas) at Joppa
- Acts 9:36-41
- Eutychus at Troas - Acts 20:6-12

HIS HEALING AND HIS AVENUES - Isa. 55:8-9; Jn.14:6; Jn. 1:1-5,14

1. Repentance & Restitution - (Prov. 28:13; Hos. 6:1)
2. Deliverance- (Obad. 1:17; Matt. 17:18; Mk. 6:13)
3. Prayers of Faith - (Matt. 21:22; Jas.5:15-16; 2Kings 20:1-6)
4. Faith in God's WORD - (Jn. 4:50,51; Acts 14:9,10)
5. Taking a Step of Faith - (Matt. 14:35-36; Lk 8:43-48)
6. Speaking Creative WORDS- (Mk.11:23; Mk.5:41;Acts9:33-34)
7. Teaching of God's WORD -(Ps. 107:20; Prov. 4:20-22;Lk 5:17)

8. Laying on of Hands -(Matt. 9:28-30; Mk. 7:32-35;Acts 28:8)
9. Anointing the Sick - (Mk. 6:13; James. 5:14)
10. Through Fasting - (Mk. 9:29; Acts 9:8-9, 17-19)
11. Partaking in the LORD'S Supper - (1 Cor. 11:29-30)
12. Gifts of the Spirit (Healing & Miracles) - (1 Cor. 12:9-10)

HIS HEALING AND ALL AFFLICTIONS- Matt. 4:23; 12:15; Ps. 34:19

1. Barrenness - (Gen.25:21-26; Lk. 1:5-25)
2. Boils - (2Kings 20:7; Job 2:7-10 ; 42:6-10)
3. Blindness - (Matt. 20:29-34; Mk. 10:46-52)
4. Deafness - (Mk. 9:25-27; Lk. 7:22)
5. Demonic Oppression - (Acts 10:38; Lk. 13:11-13)
6. Demonic Possession - (Matt. 4:24; Lk. 8:2,36)
7. Dropsy - (Lk. 14:2-4)
8. Dumbness - (Matt. 9:32-33; 12:22)
9. Fever - (Mat. 8:14-15; Acts 28:8)
10. Issue of Blood - (Matt. 9:20-22; Mk 5:25-29)

11. Lameness - (Matt. 21:14; Acts 3:2-9)
12. Leprosy - (Matt. 8:2-4; Lk. 17:11-19)
13. Lunatic (Mental illness)- (Matt. 4:24; 17:15-18)
14. Palsy (Paralysis) - (Lk. 5:18-25; Acts 9:32-34)
15. Withered Hand - (1Kings 13:4-6; Matt. 12:10-13)

CONCLUSION 1 Cor. 6:20 - " For ye are bought with a price: therefore glorify God in your body and in your spirit, which are God's" - With the price of "HIS BLOOD" lay hold on "HIS HEALING" to glorify God in your spirit, soul & body.

PRAYER POINT
Jer. 17:14 - "Heal me, O LORD, and I shall be he healed," in the name of Jesus.

LECTURE 18

THE WONDER-WORKING POWER OF THE BLOOD OF JESUS

MEMORY VERSE: He that eateth my flesh, and drinketh my blood, dwelleth in me, and I in him. John 6:56

TEXT: 1 Peter 1: 18, 19; Hebrews 10: 19-23

INTRODUCTION

In Scripture the blood is spoken of in two ways: blood shed and blood sprinkled or applied. If I ask you, what does the wonder-working power of the blood of Jesus means to you? You might answer saying,

1) it means that my sins are forgiven
2) it means that I am free from the bondage of iniquity, or
3) it means all my sins are covered by the blood of Jesus.

Yet, beyond forgiveness, what does the blood of Jesus Christ mean to you? Can you explain it to your family members or to your co-worker the value and virtue of the wonder-working power of the blood of Jesus? However, the wonder-working power of the blood of Jesus comes into effect by the sprinkling or by the application of the shed blood in our heart or situations.

I. WHAT IS IT THAT GIVES THE BLOOD OF JESUS SUCH POWER?

1. It is because the soul or life is in the blood, and that blood is offered by God on the altar, that it has in it redemptive power.
2. The soul or life is in the blood, therefore the value of the blood corresponds to the value of life that is in it.
3. When John the Baptist announced the coming of Christ, he spoke of Him as filling a dual office: as the Lamb of God that takes away the sin of the word, and as One who would baptize with the Holy Spirit. Therefore, the outpouring of the blood must take place before the outpouring of the Spirit.

II. WHAT HAS THAT POWER ACCOMPLISHED?

1. The blood of Jesus opened grave (Heb 13: 20)
2. The blood of Jesus connects us with heaven (Col. 1 : 20)
3. The blood of Jesus is all powerful in the human heart (1 Peter 1:18, 19)

4. The blood of Jesus redeems us from sin and the power of darkness (Eph. 1: 7)
5. Jesus' blood breaks down all walls (Eph. 2: 13 – 14)
6. Christ's blood overcomes Satan and put him to flight (Rev. 12: 11).
7. The blood of Jesus gives access to the Holy of Holies – to our heavenly Father - - without reproach (Heb. 10: 19)
8. The blood of Jesus cleanses us from all sin, (1 John 1 : 7 – 9)
9. The blood of Jesus is the cost of our salvation
10. The blood of Jesus gives us courage and confidence to enter the presence of God (Heb. 10: 19 – 23)
11. The blood of Jesus has made a covenant with us (Matt. 26: 26 – 28).

In summary, according to Andrew Murray, the wonder working power of the blood of Jesus has accomplished the following, among others:

12. Redemption by the blood (1 Pet. 1: 18, 19)
13. Reconciliation through the blood (Rom. 3 : 24, 25)
14. Cleansing through the blood (1 Jn 1:7)
15. Sanctification through the blood (Heb. 13 : 12)
16. Victory over Satan through the blood (Rev. 12 : 11)
17. Life in the blood (John 6: 55, 56)
18. Heavenly joy through the blood (Rev. 7: 9 – 14)
19. Cleanse by the blood to serves the living God (Eph. 2:13; Heb. 9:14)

III. HOW IS THE WONDER WORKING POWER OF THE BLOOD OF JESUS APPLIED UPON THE HEART?

1. The blood of Jesus is applied on us by the Spirit of Christ, who dwells in us - - when we receive Christ into our heart by faith (Rom. 3:25)

2. The blood of Jesus is sprinkled on our souls through the preaching of the Gospel in the power of the Holy Spirit (Acts 8 : 34 - 37)

IV. HOW CAN I KNOW WHETHER THE BLOOD OF JESUS HAS BEEN SPRINKLED UPON MY HEART?

1. If you are now willing to walk in the light and allow the Holy Spirit to expose all darkness in you, you can know you have been sprinkled (1 Jn 1:7)

2. If you call on the power of Christ's blood when you are under enemy attack, you can know you have been sprinkled.

3. When you are so secured in the cleansing, justifying power of the blood that your conscience no longer condemns you, you know you have been sprinkled. (Heb. 10: 22).

V. WHAT DOES GOD EXPECT OF US ONCE WE ARE SPRINKLED WITH THE BLOOD OF JESUS?

1. We are to go in peace - - and doubt no more (cf. Rom 5: 1)

2. We are to praise God with a thankful heart - - never doubting.

3. We are commanded to thank God for the precious blood of Jesus with high praises.

a. "And not only that, but we also rejoice in God through our Lord Jesus Christ, through whom we have now received the reconciliation" (Rom 5: 11)

b. "Be glad in the Lord and rejoice, you righteous; And shout for joy, all you upright in heart" (Ps. 32 : 11)

c. "Blessed are the people who know the joyful sound! They walk, O Lord, in the light of Your countenance"(Ps. 89 : 15)

d. "I will greatly rejoice in the Lord, My soul shall be joyful in my God; For He has clothed me with the garment of salvation, He has covered me with the robe of righteousness . .. " (Is. 61 : 10)

CONCLUSION

Be reminded that the shed blood of Jesus has never loosened its power. However, it must be sprinkled or applied upon our heart to produce its effect.

PRAYER POINTS

1. Blood of Jesus arise, purge my soul, spirit and body.

2. Blood of Jesus, arise, pursue my enemies and destroy them.

3. Blood of Jesus, arise, kill every sickness in my body

4. I break every evil covenant by the blood of Jesus.

LECTURE 19
DELIVERANCE BY THE BLOOD OF JESUS

TEXT: Ex.12:12-13; Eph.1:7; Gal.3:13-14; John 6:53; 1Pet.1:18-19; Rev.1:5-6; Rom.8:9-11.

MEMORY VERSE: Rev.12:11. And they overcame him by the blood of the Lamb, and by the word of their testimony; and they loved not their lives unto the death.

INTRODUCTION

A lot of people indulge in performing blood sacrifices, whether human or animal blood sacrifices, looking for one form of deliverance or breakthrough or protection without no guaranty of their requests being answered. The blood of Jesus, our Saviour and the Son of God is able to deliver us from any form of bondage, break yokes and free us from satan's shackles, when called upon.

ROOT POWER OF THE BLOOD OF JESUS
1. It is the blood of God; John 1:4.
2. There is life in the blood; Rom.8:2.
3. It is a sinless blood; Rom.5:19.
4. It is the blood of the renewed covenant; Heb.12:24.
5. It is blood of eternal sacrifice; Eph.5:2.

6. He is our great High Priest; Heb.3:1.
7. He is of pure divine conception; Matt.1:20.
8. The blood was shed from the foundation of the world; Rev.13:8.
9. It is the blood of divine atonement; Rom.5:11.
10. It is the blood of the Lamb without blemish; 1Pet.1:19.
11. It is the blood of the everlasting covenant; Heb.13:20.
12. He is an eternal Spirit; Heb.9:14.
13. The trinity factor; 2John1:9.

EFFICACY OF THE BLOOD OF JESUS
1. Destroys the power of sin; 1John 3:5.
2. Breaks satanic dominion; 1John 3:8.
3. Health to the flesh; Jer.30:17.
4. Protection from enemies; Ex.12:12-13.
5. Shield from destruction; Col.1:14.
6. Breaks the power of oppression; Rom.5:9.
7. Removes infirmities; Isa.53:3-5;
8. Destroys the works of witchcraft.

THE POWER IN THE BLOOD OF JESUS

9. Blocks accidents.
10. Stops demonic influx; Acts 19:14.
11. Paralyses wicked spirits; Rev.12:11.
12. Silences evil voices.
13. Disgraces demons.
14. Breaks curses; Gal.3:13.
15. Breaks covenants; Heb.8:6.
16. Cancels spells.
17. Pulls down evil thoughts; 2Cor.10:4.
18. Speaks good things; Heb.12:24.
19. Revokes evil prophesies.
20. Silences witchcraft incantations.
21. Protects from evil arrows.
22. Breaks the power of evil habits.
23. Clear spiritual visions.
24. Resurrects dead things; John 6:54.
25. Immunity; John 6:56.
26. Destroying the power of enchantment; Num.23:23.
27. Destroying the power of bewitchment; Num.23:23.
28. A spiritual insecticide against wicked roaming spirits.

HINDERANCES TO THE EFFECTIVENESS OF THE BLOOD

1. Lack of love; 1John2:10-11.
2. Bitterness; Eph.4:31.
3. Unforgiveness; Mark 11:26.
4. Pleasures of sin; Heb.11:25.
5. Perpetual disobedience; Tit.1:16.
6. Idols in the heart; Eze.14:3.
7. Backsliding.
8. Clever and wilful sinners; 2Tim.2:19.
9. Love of money; 1Tim6:10.
10. Those who have become obstacles in the house of God; Mark 9:42.
11. Tongues that commit murder at will; Prov.6:16.
12. Those who operate under suspicion rather than revelation; Col.3:12-13.
13. Hypocrites; Matt.7:23.
14. Anyone who hates his fellow brethren; 1John 4:20.
15. Those who ask for grace but are not ready to forsake their sins; Rom.6:1.
16. Those who see the church as a business place rather than an eternity function; 2Cor.11:26.
17. Those who are quick to judge other people's weaknesses but fail to see their own weaknesses.

18. Those who create divisions in the house of God.
19. Those with lustful hearts.
20. Doubting the potency of the blood of Jesus.
21. Ignorance of the effectiveness of the blood.
22. Those who practice wickedness.

HOW TO BENEFIT FROM THE DELIVERANCE POWER OF THE BLOOD

1. You must be convicted and then converted; Matt.8:3.
2. Confession and repentance; Matt.3:8, 2Pet.3:9.
3. Must become a believer in words and actions; 1Tim.4:12.
4. Regular prayer and bible study; 2Pet.3:18.
5. Pleading the Blood of Jesus regularly.
6. Soaking you in the Blood of Jesus daily.
7. Separate yourself from false brethren; 2Tim.3:3-5.
8. Live a holy life; Rom.12:1.
9. Pray in the Spirit; Eph.6:10.

CONCLUSION

The shedding of the blood of Jesus brought about salvation and also deliverance. Satan's gift to mankind is bondage, destruction, violence, famine but ultimately eternal damnation. Glory be to God for deliverance, not by the blood of animals but by the blood of Jesus shed over 2000 years ago, but still the blood of Jesus is available, ever-ready and fully loaded.

PRAYER POINTS

1. Blood of Jesus make me whole, in Jesus name.

2. Blood of Jesus fight for me, in Jesus name.

3. Blood of Jesus speak for me in the camp of my enemies, in Jesus name.

LECTURE 20

WHAT THE SCRIPTURE SAYS ABOUT THE BLOOD OF JESUS

MEMORY VERSE(S): "..He expounded unto them in ALL the scripture the things concerning himself....having obtained eternal redemption for us by His own BLOOD - Luke 24:27; Heb. 9:12

TEXT(S): Zech. 9:11,12; Jn. 6:53-58; Heb. 9:11-15; 10:19-22

INTRODUCTION

When God "made coats of skins, and clothed" Adam and Eve (Gen. 3:21), he was saying that their Sins can only be covered by shedding blood, so, "Blood Sacrifices" were the means of access into His presence and the basis of fellowship with him, for "without shedding of blood is no remission" of Sins (Heb. 9:22). "SIN" - is the problem and "BLOOD" is the redemption price to buy us back from the consequence of sin which is "DEATH" (Rom. 6:23). It is written that "the life of the flesh is in the blood: and ...it is the blood that maketh atonement for the soul" (Lev. 17:11). This implies that "life must be "laid down" or forfeited in payment for sin - and this is exactly what Jesus did for the whole human race (Jn.1:29; 10:17,18; 19:30).

This principle of usage of "life" (blood) for the atonement of sin runs through the whole Scripture (i.e the Bible). For an in-depth study and thorough analysis of "what the scripture says about the blood of Jesus", we'll be looking at the following sub-topic:

1. The Principle of His Blood
2. The Purpose of His Blood
3. The Purity of His Blood
4. The Perfection of His Blood
5. The Power of His Blood
6. The Privileges of His Blood
7. The Partakers of His Blood

THE PRINCIPLE OF HIS BLOOD

Heb. 9:22 - "without shedding of Blood is no remission"

1. **Adam** - "unto Adam also and to his wife did the LORD God make coat of skins and clothed them. - Gen. 3:21. ·After a blood sacrifice to remit their sins, God used the skin of that innocent animal to cloth them. This is a type of the blood of Jesus.

2. **Abel** - "By faith Abel offered unto God a more excellent sacrifice than cain...he

brought of the firstling of his flock. - Heb. 11:4; Gen. 4:4. *The faith of "blood sacrifice" of a lamb, a type of Jesus Christ, brought righteousness to Abel.

3. **Abraham** - "By faith Abraham,...offered up Isaac..And he said, My son, God will provide himself a l a m b for a burnt offering.."Heb. 11:17-19;Gen. 22:7,8. *The faith of offering Isaac, the most precious possession Abraham had, brought a miracle Ram for Blood sacrifice", a type of the blood of Jesus.

4. **A Passover Lamb** - "Your lamb shall be without blemish..kill it..take of the blood, & strike it on the 2 side posts &upper doorpost of the house.. and when I see the BLOOD, I will pass over you.." Ex. 12:5-7, 13. *That Passover lamb was symbolic of the sacrifice of the blood of Jesus, the lamb of God (Jn. 1:29)

5. **A Sucking Lamb** - "Samuel took a sucking lamb, & offered it for a burnt offering wholly unto the LORD.." 1 Sam. 7:7-10. *The offering of Samuel

was on behalf of Israel against the philistines so, God to smote them.This is a type of the blood of Jesus,the lamb of God.

6. **The Smitten Rock** -"And the LORD said unto moses..take thy rod..and thou shalt smite the rock and there shall come water out of it.. and that Rock was Christ" Ex.17:5,6; 1Cor. 10:4. *The smiting of the Rock was a type of the sacrifice of Jesus for "He was smitten of God" (Isa. 53:4). The smitting speaks of "Crucifixion", the cross. When Jesus was smitten, "water" & Blood came from his side.

7. **The Lifted Serpent** - "And as Moses lifted up the Serpent in the wilderness, even so must the son of man be lifted up; that whosoever believeth in him should not perish, but have eternal life. - Jn. 3:14,15. * Jesus likened his assignment as our "Saviour" to that of a "Serpent". A serpent is a type of "SIN", so "God made him a sin for us"(2Cor. 5:21) by lifting Him up on the cross for a blood sacrifice for remission of our "SINS".

THE PURPOSE OF HIS BLOOD

Gen. 3:15; Matt. 1:21; 1 Jn. 3:8; Jn. 10:10; Isa. 9:6-7

1. Redemption -
(i) From sin & its consequences - (Matt. 1:21; Tit. 2:14; 1Jn. 3:8)
(ii) From the power of Darkness - (Zech. 9:11-12; Lk. 1:74; Col. 1:13)
(iii) From the wrath to come - (Rom. 5:9; 1 Thess. 1:10; 5:9)
2. Restoration -
(i) Back to Edenic Fellowship - (Gen. 3:8-10; 1 Jn. 1:3,7; Phil. 2:1)
(ii) Back to Edenic Fruitfulness - (Gen.1:26-28;Isa.51:3; Rev.5:12)
(iii) Back to Edenic Family - (Gen.2:18-25; Mal. 2:13-16;Matt.19:3-9)
3. Reigning -
(i) As Heirs of God - (Rom. 8:17; Gal. 4:7)
(ii) As Kings & Priests -(Rev. 1:6; 5:10)
(iii) As Millennium Rulers - (Rev. 20:4,6)

THE PURITY OF HIS BLOOD

Ex. 12:5-7,13; Lev. 1:10-11; Jn. 1:29; 8:46; Heb. 9:14

1. He was one of the Trinity from eternity (Col. 1:15-17; 1 Jn. 5:7)

2. He was conceived of the Holy Ghost. (Matt 1:20, Lk. 1:35)
3. He was righteous, hating wickedness (Ps. 45:7; Isa. 42:6)
4. He was faultless before the Pilate (Lk. 23:4; Jn. 18:38; 19:4,6)
5. His Blood was called "the innocent Blood" (Matt. 27:4)
6. He was referred to as the "Holy Child Jesus" (Acts 4:27)
7. He was called "the Holy one of God" (Mk. 1:24; Lk. 4:34)
8. He nevercommitted any sin (Jn. 8:46; 1 Pet. 2:22)
9. His priesthood was without any defilement (Heb. 4:15; 7:26)
10. He was without blemish and without spot. (1 Pet. 1:19;1 Jn. 3:5)

THE PERFECTION OF HIS BLOOD

Lev. 14:7; Ps. 12:6; Heb. 10:14; 1 Jn. 5:8

"Jesus shed His Blood SEVEN TIMES to grant us freedom&deliverance from sin, its consequences & all the works of devil".

1. His Blood was shed as they "plucked off" His beard.-Isa. 50:6

2. His Blood was shed as he "sweated" during prayers - Luke22:44
3. His Blood was shed when they put a "crown of thorns'" upon His head - Matt. 27:29
4. His Blood was shed when they scourged Him. And with each "stripe", blood was drawn from Him. " - Matt. 27:26
5. His Blood was shed when they "pierced'His hands. - Ps. 22:16
6. His Blood was shed when they "pierced" His feet. - Ps. 22:16
7. His Blood was shed along with water, when a Soldier "Pierced" His side with a spear. "Jn 19:34

THE POWER OF HIS BLOOD

Jn. 6:56; Col. 1:13-14; 1Jn. 1:7-10; Rev. 12:11

1. Access to the Holiest - Heb. 10:19; Eph. 2:13
2. Cleansing - 1 Jn. 1:7; Rev. 1:5; 7:14
3. Deliverance - Zech. 9:11-12; Col. 1:13
4. Eternal Life - Jn. 6:53-54, 57
5. Forgiveness - Eph. 1:7; Col. 1:14
6. Healing - Isa. 53:5; 1 Pet. 2:24
7. Justification - Rom. 5:9; 3:24

8. Peace with God - Rom. 5:1; Col. 1:20
9. Protection - Jn. 6:56; Ps. 91:1
10. Purged Conscience - Heb. 9:14
11. Reconciliation - 2Cor. 5:18-19; Col. 1:20
12. Redemption - Heb. 9:12; Rev. 5:9
13. Righteousness - Rom. 3:25-26
14. Sanctification - Heb. 13:12; 1 Pet. 1:2
15. Victory - Rev. 12:11; 1 Cor. 15:57

THE PRIVILEGES OF HIS BLOOD

Heb. 9:12,15; Rev. 5:1-12 "the promise of eternal inheritance".

1. **Power** - (Ps. 110:2; Lk. 10:19; Acts 1:8)
2. **Riches** - (Deut.8:18; Ps. 112:1-3; 2Cor. 8:9)
3. **Wisdom** - (Prov. 4:7; Lk. 21:15; Eph. 3:10)
4. **Strength** - (Isa. 40:31; Lk. 22:31,32; Phil. 4:13)
5. **Honour** - (1 Sam. 2:30; Prov. 4:8; Jn.12:26)
6. **Glory** - (Prov. 4:9; Rom. 8:30; 1 Pet.5:10)
7. **Blessing** - (Prov. 10:22; Eph. 1:3; 1 pet. 3:9)

THE PARTAKERS OF HIS BLOOD

Jn. 6:53-55; Heb.10:19; 4:16; 1 Jn. 5:7,8

1. Decide-To be "a new creature". (Jn.3:3;Rom.10:9,10;2Cor.5:17)
2. Determine -To "be Holy" (Heb. 10:19-23, 12:14; 1Pet 1:15,16)
3. Develop - "Desire growth" (Acts. 20:32; Heb. 10:25; Jude 1:20)
4. Deliverance - "Desire freedom" (Mk. 16:17; Lk. 4:18; Jn. 8:32)
5. Dine - In "communion Service" (Jn. 6:53-56; 1 Cor. 10:17)
6. Decree - To "Sprinkle" His Blood. (Num. 14:28; Heb. 12:24)
7. Defence - "Fight of Faith" (Matt. 11:12; Eph. 6:12; 1 Tim. 6:12)

CONCLUSION:

Having therefore brethren, boldness to enter into THE HOLIEST by the BLOOD OF JESUS;..let us draw near with a true heart..for He is faithful that promised. -Heb. 10:19-23

PRAYER POINT:

(Zech. 9:11) - Blood of Jesus, arise and deliver me from every pit of the wicked, in the name of Jesus.

LECTURE 21

CLEANSING THROUGH THE BLOOD OF JESUS

Memory Verse: 1 John 1:7 "But if we walk in the light, as he is in the light, we have fellowship one with another, and the Blood of Jesus Christ his son cleanseth us from all sin."

INTRODUCTION

The Blood of Jesus is grossly misunderstood because of the mysteries it carries. It is not an ordinary blood but, the blood of the only begotten son of God (JOHN 3: 16, Lev.17:11). The subject of 'CLEANSING BLOOD' begins in Genesis and keeps running like a never-ending stream, reaching the highest point in the book of Revelation. Some of the great verses in the bible have to do with atoning (Lev. 17:11), cleansing (Jer., 33:8, Ezekiel 37:23), saving (Eph.1:7) efficacious and redeeming blood of our Lord Jesus (Rev. 1:5).

Meaning of Words
To 'cleanse' means to make clean, pure, to wash, to bathe, to purify, without blemish or spot:
(a) from physical stains and dirt, as in the case of utensils, Matt. 23:256

(b) In a moral sense, from defilement of sin. James 4:8 2 Cor. 7:1
(c) From the guilt of sin. Eph. 5:26, 1 John 1:7
(d) To pronounce clean in a 'Levitical sense' Mark 7:19, Acts 10:15
(e) To consecrate by cleansings, Heb 9:22, 23: 10:2

Blood sacrifices in the Old Testament

Blood sacrifices were used throughout the Old Testament as an important part of the people's lives before God and the following lessons could be learnt from them:
(1) The importance of the shedding of blood and need for sacrifice to be made for sin.

(2) The concept of substitution.

(3) Atonement for sin
But ALL of these pointed to Jesus and His work. (Hebrew 9:22

THE MYSTERY OF ATONEMENT AND REMISSION OF SINS.

Hebrew 9:9, 11-15

There is a major difference between the Blood of the New Covenant and the Blood of Old Covenant. In the Old Testament, animal sacrifices were made to 'atone' for people's sins. Exodus 30:10, Leviticus 16:11-17, 17:11. What atonement did then was to cover sin but did not take sin away, as the guilt remained in people's conscience as they were still aware it. Hebrew 10:1-4. Under the New Covenant, the Blood of Jesus completely washes us from sin, and not only that we have remission – a complete wiping out of sin as though it had never been. Christ offered us an "eternal redemption" vs. 12, cleansing of conscience, vs. 14, thus removing the guilt and condemnation of it from the heart.

TYPES OF CLEANSING

Cleansing: By water – Ezekiel 36:25
By blood – Rev., 1:5
By fire – Malachi 3:3

THE CLEANSING POWER OF THE BLOOD

1. It cleanses from past sins. Isaiah 44:22, 43:25, Psalm 103:12, 79:8, Micah 7:19
2. It cleanses from all present sins. 1 John 1:7-9
3. It cleanses from all possible sins. 1 John 2: 1-2
4. It cleanses from power of sin. Romans 6 :1-2
5. It cleanses from the penalty of sin. 1 Pet., 18-19

There are two kinds of sin that the blood of Jesus deals with powerfully, both kinds of sin are cleansed by the blood of Jesus, but, the blood is activated differently in each case:

- The sin that is confessed and forsaken. (1 John 1:9) and
- The sin that we are not aware of as we walk in the light. (1John 1:7)

NB: The Blood of Jesus only cleanses sin, but doesn't cleanse excuses. Covering up achieves nothing, but confession brings cleansing.

THE POWER IN THE BLOOD OF JESUS

BLESSINGS OF CLEANSING

- Assurance of Salvation - (Romans 5: 8-9)
- Fellowship: (1 John 1:3)
- Pure Heart (Mat .5:8, 1Tim. 1:5,)
- Pure Conscience (Heb. 10:2)
- Access to God (Eph 3:12 , 2:18)
- Reconciliation and Restoration (Romans 5:10-11)
- Right standing with God(Eph.1:5)
- Sonship (Gal.4:7)
- Joint -Heirs with Christ (Romans 8:17)
- Heavenly-bound- Rev.

Conditions for Enjoying the Blessings:

- Adequate Knowledge of the cleansing power in the blood of Jesus.
- Great desire to appropriate the blessings.
- Strong willingness to separate yourself from everything that is unclean.
- Exercising faith in the power of the Blood.

Conclusion:

The Blood of Jesus is a powerful agent for cleansing of sin. It is God's solution for sin that is more powerful than the sin. In Christ our sins, our past is gone, completely washed away as if it never existed. God has no more remembrance of it, and if we fully understand the cleansing power of the Blood of Jesus, we will be free from guilt and condemnation of those sins. Something that is new has no past! Praise GOD!!!

Then, we can joyfully sing Hymn 55 from our Gospel Hymn Book: To God be the glory great things He hath done!

Made in the USA
Lexington, KY
04 October 2015